THE FARCE OF

MASTER PIERRE PATELIN

Composed by an unknown Author about 1469 A. D.

Englished by RICHARD HOLBROOK

Illustrated with facsimiles of
the woodcuts in the edition of
PIERRE LEVET, Paris, *ca.* 1489

BOSTON AND NEW YORK
HOUGHTON MIFFLIN AND COMPANY
THE RIVERSIDE PRESS CAMBRIDGE
MDCCCCV

Maiſtre pierre pathelin

The emblem of Pierre Levet

To my friends
WILLIAM LYON PHELPS
and
WILLIAM ALBERT NITZE

CONTENTS

Preface . . . . ix–xv

Setting of the Comédie Française . . xvii–xix

Introduction . . . . . xxi–xxxviii

The Text 1–94

Notes on the Text 95–112

Notes on the Cuts 113–116

LIST OF ILLUSTRATIONS

The emblem of Pierre Levet . . . *Frontispiece*

Patelin, counting on his fingers 7

It is too much 15

The Draper visits Patelin 33

The Shepherd comes to explain . . . 61

The court scene 71

Patelin tries to collect his fee 91

[vii]

PREFACE

ALL that I have to say of *Patelin* as a work of literature will be found in the Introduction or in the Notes on the Text. It is not amiss therefore to make here certain remarks of a more dry and technical nature.

This translation was made from my manuscript copy of the only known extant exemplar of the *Patelin* printed by Guillaume Le Roy* at Lyons, about 1486. Before December 20, 1490,† Le Roy's *Patelin* was faithfully reprinted, with six excellent illustrative woodcuts, by Pierre Levet, a celebrated Parisian printer and publisher. Of Levet's *Patelin*, also, only one exemplar is now believed to exist. This book, which is preserved at the Bibliothèque Nationale in Paris, is a beautiful specimen

---

* Lent me by its generous owner, M. Albert Rosset of Lyons, France.

† See my essay on '*Maître Patelin* in the Gothic editions by Pierre Levet and Germain Beneaut,' in *Modern Philology* for June, 1905.

of early printing, and is fortunately in perfect condition. I say 'fortunately' because several pages have at some indefinite period been lost from the older *Patelin* by Le Roy. These are now replaced by pen-and-ink counterfeits, probably derived from Levet, and executed so skilfully as almost to escape detection.

From the fifteenth century only one manuscript has come down. Whether or not this manuscript is earlier than Le Roy's edition, it offers a less authoritative text, and only one of its readings has been followed in this translation. But, since Le Roy's edition is probably the first, and as it is hardly more than seventeen years younger than the farce itself (*ca.* 1469), there is no reason to suppose that it differs essentially from the author's manuscript, which, no doubt, was long ago thumbed out of existence by the first actors who performed his masterpiece.

It may be interesting to know how Fournier's version of this farce is arranged for production at the Comédie Française. It is divided into three acts. The first ends with the Draper's soliloquy, Scene iv (lines 344–351). The second act begins, therefore, with Scene v. Scene vi, except the words 'Hello! Master Pierre!' spoken by the Draper a moment after he has knocked at Patelin's door, must be omitted. The Draper's soliloquy at the end of Scene VIII will be uttered before he quits Patelin's bedroom.

Pursuing this system, we must omit Scene X and Scene XII, though we hear the Draper pounding angrily on Patelin's door, and distinguish the words 'Ho, there! mis'ess: where are you hiding?' Next, the Draper must speak the lines of Scene XIV, not in the street, but at Patelin's, as a kind of soliloquy.

Act III begins with Scene XVI. As the Shepherd leaves him, the Draper disappears within his shop; then the Shepherd, instead of going to Patelin's house and calling, 'Is any one within?' meets Patelin as that worthy comes strolling across the market-place, and accosts him because he recognises by Patelin's dress that he is a lawyer. We must now give the Shepherd an exit after his last lines in Scene XVII; he will reappear, somewhere in the crowd, about as the Judge asks, 'Where is the defendant? Is he present in person?' shortly after the beginning of the trial scene. From this point onward the piece proceeds precisely as it did when it was first performed.

In the text of my translation hardly any of these suggestions for rearrangement occur; for they are purely modern and would often contradict the other set of stage-directions which are reasonably derived from study of the text. These are largely my own, though many of them are due to my notes on a performance of Fournier's version at the Comédie Française in August, 1904.

Elsewhere (pages xvii–xix) will be found a pretty accurate description of the stage-setting adopted by the Comédie Française. Absolute accuracy is something I am far from claiming; for while the play was in progress the pit was rather dim, and I was too fascinated to be taking notes.

In the oldest texts of *Patelin* there is but one stage-direction (see Notes on the Text, Note v), and there is no division into acts or scenes; nor are the verses numbered.

As to costume nothing need be said; for M. Boutet de Monvel's sixteen dry-point etchings show admirably how the various personages in our farce would have been dressed about the year 1470. In the fourth volume of his work on *Le Costume Historique*, Racinet gives a lithographic reproduction of a fifteenth-century miniature showing what colours might be worn by a Judge, his Clerk, a Lawyer, and a Bailiff (or *Sergent à verge*), etc., in the second half of the fifteenth century. This lithograph is a copy of a French manuscript marked 'Ancien fonds 9387' and preserved at the Bibliothèque Nationale. The miniature is no doubt an accurate representation of a court scene of that period. But the court scene in *Patelin*

[xii]

may reasonably be supposed to occur in a market-place.

As we learn from the opening conversation be-tween Patelin and Guillemette, their clothes are threadbare; and as the Shepherd says (to Patelin), 'even though I be ill clad,' we may safely assume that his apparel was mostly in rags.

The six illustrative woodcuts which Pierre Levet published with his *Patelin* about 1489 are offered in facsimile with this translation. These woodcuts were undoubtedly made especially for Levet's edition, and were not borrowed, with little or no sense of fitness, from some earlier work, as com-monly happened in the infancy of printing. They are valuable for two reasons: in the first place they are almost contemporaneous with our farce, and show, however crudely, what the illustrator, or illustrators (for there may have been two), fancied to have been the looks of five characters whose likes could be observed at any time; in the second place, these woodcuts are no doubt the first that were ever made to illustrate for the printing-press a comedy composed in a modern tongue. Do they prove anything as to the use of stage scenery? Or are we to believe their setting is purely conventional, chosen merely because the engraver did not care to sketch figures in the air? The question is hard to answer, yet I am con-

[xiii]

vinced that the farces *were not performed on empty platforms;* the 'serious drama' was staged with complicated machinery, and it is hardly reasonable to suppose that the farces, which grew out of the 'serious drama' and were often performed with it, could have lacked all scenery, or that they had, forsooth, no other setting than a wall, a floor, a bench and a chair. No archæological proof exists to compel conscientious moderns to adopt a sceneless stage in performing medieval comedies; on the other hand, art does not require that they be elaborately staged, with gorgeous scenery such as is generally used to make Shakespere's plays seem more plausible to persons whose imaginations can not perceive the temple-haunting martlet amid his lov'd mansionry.

Now, as to this translation. To the best of my belief no other English translation of *Patelin* has ever been printed. Thus there was no model, either to help or to harm ; nor was there, furthermore, any adequate dictionary to quicken the pace. I cannot say, as Shelton said of his *Don Quixote*, that I did this work in forty days. It has taken nearer twenty months, and in this case it is not at all true that 'le temps ne fait rien à l'affaire'; for *Patelin* teems with difficulties, — some of them so great that perhaps they may never be solved, while others yield their secret only after one has ransacked a dozen volumes for the answer. Of course the commentators* help, especially when they are scholars like Mr. Kristoffer Nyrop or the late Gaston Paris, but in the main the translator has had to make his way alone, then retrace his steps a score of times, smoothing his path little by little, until he concludes at last that further efforts on his part are vain. He is a pioneer and knows perfectly well that some day the work will be better done.

* Génin's edition, published in 1854, should not be forgotten. Génin put forth several theories whose falsity could hardly have failed to be evident to some of his contemporaries, and not only his text, but also his commentary, contains many inaccuracies ; yet Génin, despite his whimsies, was a clever man, and his edition deserved the recognition accorded to it by Littré and Renan. Ample allowance must be made for the fact that Romance philology was at that time a new science.

Paul Lacroix published his edition of *Patelin* in 1859. Lacroix made some improvements in the text, but his notes, often derived from Génin, show no great advance, and are marred by their facetious abuse of Génin.

THE STAGE-SETTING OF
THE COMÉDIE FRANÇAISE

(With some stage-directions)

ACT I

A MARKET–PLACE, such as one might have seen in a small French town about the year 1469. To the left, a low building of which two sides are partly visible. This is the shop of the draper Guillaume Joceaulme, whose name is written in large Gothic letters over the heavy double door. Behind this shop, but separated from it by a lane, stands a dwelling whose roof rises from several gables to various peaks, joined by decorative ridges. A little further to the right, in the distant background, stands a church tower, skirted on the left by a narrow street which is lost to view among the houses that lean over it and straggle along its sides. In the foreground, half concealing the church tower, is a stone canopy, or market-cross, whose roof rises steeply to a stone tuft, like the finial of a cathedral.

In each of the four sides of this structure is a niche with a stone seat. The only seat visible will be occupied by the Judge during the trial scene. The whole canopy rests on masonry so disposed as to form six or seven steps on all four sides.

In the foreground to the right, facing the shop of Guillaume, is a stone dwelling, and beyond it, in the background, are other buildings through which runs a street so narrow and tortuous that it is soon lost to view in an uncertain mass of houses which separate it from the church.

In the foreground, between the market-cross and the Draper's shop, stands a short thick post on which rests a box with a slot in it to admit the God's-pennies of those who trade in the market-place.

When the curtain rises on this Gothic scene the townsfolk are just beginning to bestir themselves for the day's business and the glow of morning is visible over the housetops, though the light has not illuminated the crooked lanes. There are vague noises; an apprentice opens the Draper's shop, brings out a table, and upon this counter he sets about arranging some of his master's goods in orderly piles. Presently Master Pierre Patelin emerges from the street to the left,

followed by his wife Guillemette. The lawyer is
bent in meditation. As he slowly enters the market-place he begins to speak to Guillemette.

ACT II

A room in Patelin's house. In the left wall is
a door opening on the street. Against the rear
wall stands a bedstead with a tester whose curtains
reach the floor and may be drawn so as to hide the
bed completely. Near the bed and the door is
a great armchair. In the wall to the right is a window through which enters a rather dim light. Before this window stands a heavy wooden table,
very plain, and close to the table is an ordinary
chair. Though the room looks tidy enough,
everything about it bears witness to poverty.

ACT III

The Draper's shop is closed; otherwise the
same setting as for Act I.

INTRODUCTION

PATELIN belongs to a series of farces which had come mysteriously into being as early as 1277, when a little piece called *The Boy and the Blind Man* was performed at Tournay.* Most of these farces have been lost, but the hundred and fifty or so that happen to

---

* If not in 1277, at all events about that time. This tiny farce was discovered by M. Paul Meyer some forty years ago. Of the farces extant two score were found by some one rummaging in a Berlin attic about 1840. *The Boy and the Blind Man* owes its preservation to the happy chance that some scribe saw fit to copy it at the end of a manuscript containing the *Roman d' Alexandre.*

This farce is no shapeless embryo, but shows, on the contrary, that farce-makers must have been plying their trade as early, at least, as 1250. The theme of *The Boy and the Blind Man* is picaresque. An urchin offers to lead a blind man, whose trustfulness he rewards by robbery and violence ; but, like Molière's Scapin, the boy contrives to make his victim believe that some third person is guilty.

Two comic plays by Adam de la Hale belong to the same period, but they could scarcely be called farces.

survive show clearly enough what must have been the character and range of all.

The old farces breathe the scandal and mockery of their time. Seldom if ever do they rise to a height from which man can be seen in his relation to the world. They reek of a cold sensuality into which love never enters. They are nearly all devoid of the humour which accompanies a Molière's insight into the weaknesses of man and the vagaries of society. Like most modern farces they deal with fads, rather than with the great movements of their time. No extant farce alludes unmistakeably to Jeanne d'Arc: she belonged to an earlier age than that in which she was born; but women with almost no redeeming quality abound, and are portrayed with a coarseness of feeling and an indelicacy of language for which occasional wit cannot atone. Graceful irony, irony like that of the *Franc-archer de Bagnolet*, is rare. There are no heroes and no heroines, no brave actions and no leaders; but plenty of rogues and fools, whose guile and folly give rise to those situations which picaresque literature swarms with and which had once delighted the makers of *fabliaux*. But these situations are realistic, almost invariably, and modern. Whether the farces are base or not, we of the twentieth century should find it easier to talk with their authors than with the bards who two or three centuries earlier had sung of war and romance.

When the farces began to flourish, chivalry was rapidly going out of fashion; the modern world of business and practical ideas was coming in; the bourgeois had ousted the knight, and having money to spend, he spent it on purveyors who were ready to tell him about himself and his neighbours. The town-crier gave him some news, but that was not highly spiced; real journalists were still unknown. At the theatre, and there only, could he get reflections of life. It mattered little whether these reflections were false; whether they were due to sheer second-hand glimpses, so to speak, cast into disreputable corners, never resting on life's broad avenues; he craved sensation, he liked heightened scenes based on contemporary gossip or contemporary facts, flavoured with scandal, something credible but seemingly not commonplace.

In the long-winded mysteries he could witness the spectacular performance of biblical scenes from the Creation to the Crucifixion, or of scenes derived from later history and legend. The miracle-plays manifested the power of Our Lady or of some saint, intervening in behalf of a medieval or earlier celebrity on the brink of perdition. In both these types thoroughly popular scenes abounded. Many specimens of the 'serious drama' contain comic episodes, different, however, from those of the farces. In the Middle Ages the Devil inspired terror, but he was also closely akin to the mountebank. Hence his presence on the medieval stage. Clad in skins of beasts, or in other fantastic garb, he and his imps performed antics both fearful and grotesque.

The moralities were commonly didactic, and dealt, like *Everyman*, with abstractions, such as Gluttony and the five senses, Lust, Learning, or Better-than-before; the *sotties* are mainly claptrap satirical dialogues showing little or no plot and composed for clowns or *sots*, who enlivened their garrulous banter by performing acrobatic feats. These *sotties* were written in verse, but otherwise they closely resemble the medleys of dialogue, song, and gymnastics to be found nowadays at almost any music-hall.

With the *sotties* and the moralities the farces have a great deal in common, so much, sometimes, that one can hardly distinguish between them; but the farces are generally more like life, and there are some reasons for believing that they were more popular.* In them the bourgeois saw

* This Introduction merely glimpses into the history of medieval drama. Mr. E. K. Chambers has gathered an immense mass of information in his two volumes on *The Medieval Stage*, Oxford, 1903, and Mr. J. Mortensen's very readable book on

[xxiv]

images of his existence, and though the reflection of reality often resembles the distorted figures beheld in some old-fashioned mirror, never before had literature come so near to the facts of life in its homely phases. Like some modern reprobate who was flattered to find a grossly realistic caricature of himself in a comic paper, many a citizen of the fifteenth century, happening to find himself travestied in a farce, could have said, *Cet ignoble individu, c'est moi!* The farces were, in fact, the only form of art that enabled him to witness household or other familiar scenes, and little as the average truth was like the theatrical representation, his enjoyment was immense. Through eye and ear he could relish depravity with nothing more than a mental participation in the sin. Here was an offset to the humdrum round. At church he could hear the parish priest chant psalms and pray for the cure of souls; at the theatre he might catch him in merrier business, conniving with crafty housewives to gull their husbands, and sinning as often as he could get a chance to sin. Here foolish rich men were regularly bamboozled by sly ' galants '; merchants cheated and were cheated in their turn; fools gave rein to their folly; everybody was tempted and fell. The whole middle-class world,

Le théâtre français au moyen âge, Paris, 1903, also deals with facts.

and sometimes nobles or churls, had an opportunity to be vividly ridiculous.

In these old farces vice almost always gets the better of virtue; thinking is mostly scheming; love is mere feigning; truth is boldly sacrificed to mirth, and mirth is the aim of all. No wonder that Bossuet, finding the same old *esprit gaulois* alive in Molière, called him an 'infamous histrion.' Nor is it in the least astonishing that a parish priest, and later the Archbishop of Paris, refused to allow Molière's body to be buried in consecrated ground. These ecclesiastics were merely keeping up a tradition which their predecessors had established when the farce-makers, indifferent as to the morality of their *dramatis personae*, were charged with undoing the work of the Church. There is, indeed, no reason to suppose that the old farces increased either piety or goodness, however much they may have amused their hearers and sharpened their wits.

He who seeks to build a history of manners out of such material must be wary indeed; for the farces display a perverted interest in special aspects of vice and folly in the lower and middle classes, or their familiars, rather than in all contemporary life. But they record the every-day language of their time. Without them to help us, we should not know a wide variety of oaths, slang, saws, superstitions, and so forth; had the specimens that survive been lost, the habits and every-day thoughts of the fourteenth, fifteenth, and early sixteenth centuries would be even further beyond our ken than now.

The old farces were always composed in octosyllabic rime, are written in a conversational style, and they are never poetical. They are for the most part brief, not a third as long as *Patelin*. Sometimes one finds a neatly constructed plot, and ingenious situations are not lacking; but in general they are flimsily constructed and seem more like dramatised anecdotes than like true drama; natural motives are too often absent, and their psychology is not so accurate as that which our modern farces commonly display, yet the dialogue is often lively and produces an adequate illusion.

From what has been said it need not be supposed that shallowness was universal; for Villon knew himself, at least, and embodied his wayward, passionate, will-less life in lyric verse which for vividness and sincerity surpasses all other lyric poetry written in his time or in the Middle Ages. He is the most gifted poet of the fifteenth century, as the author of *Patelin* is its most gifted dramatist. The historian Commines was another shrewd observer of his fellow men, and these are not all. Great, too, though the defects of the farces are, they show a keener appreciation of reality and a greater gift of natural expression than had been shown by any other form of medieval literature composed in France, save, perhaps, the realistic passages in certain *nouvelles*, in the 'serious drama,' in Villon, and in Adam de la Hale.

The farces must have arisen pretty early in the thirteenth century; in the fourteenth century, and even till the middle of the fifteenth, they seem to have languished; for farce-makers could not thrive amid war and waste. The relatively prosperous times that followed the Hundred Years' War were their Golden Age; but the Renaissance, with its Plautus and Terence, who for some twelve centuries had been preserved by monks more capable of copying manuscripts than of understanding them, brought new ideals. Playwrights began to forsake the market-place and the farces grew fewer and fewer, though the writing of them never wholly ceased. When they lost their hold, most of them perished; hardly a manuscript is left, and only a few were chosen when the early printers began to search for entertaining matter amid the ruck of the Middle Ages.

Patelin distinctly belongs to the *genre*, but in every regard it excels all other extant farces. The author of this piece, whoever he may have been and wherever he may have lived, was a genius, and

[xxviii]

when he wrote it he was inspired. Remote as he must ever remain from us, we know that he was not remote from his own time. He catches its spirit and embodies that spirit in forms whose first words cast the spell of illusion which is essential to all dramatic art.

Whether the author of *Patelin* cared deeply about morals is an unsolvable riddle. Michelet declares somewhere that *Patelin* is the 'epic of an age of rogues'; unquestionably rogues are its heroes and their rascality is its theme. If that 'practical' monarch Louis XI* ever saw *Patelin* performed — and nothing undemonstrable is more likely — how keenly he must have relished its common sense, its mirthful and remorseless roguery! We may imagine his laughter as he saw one rascal outwit another, until a mere lout, a 'sheep in clothing,' outwits them all. That was something after his own heart. We need not regard the five worthies of our farce as disciples of Louis XI: they are more than that, for they express what is unloveable in that century more plainly than does the King. They represent in several distinct and ludicrous phases the poverty, the greed, the cynical cunning, the selfishness, and the grinning depravity characteristic of the fifteenth century, at least in France.

* See Ernest Renan's essay on *Patelin* in his *Essais de morale et de critique*, 1859.

Patelin is a shabby pettifogger; his successful fellow barristers are arrayed, as he says, in silks and satins, *de camelos . . . et de camocas;* but the apparel is nothing : the lawyers are mostly rogues. And so is our Judge: he cares little about dealing out justice and he invites Patelin to sup with him, though that lawyer has spent a Saturday in the stocks. The Draper is both greedy and sly ; the Shepherd is a numbskull with a highly developed bump of villainy. And what is Guillemette? A receiver of stolen goods. Not one of these types has any sense of right. Their morality, as Renan says, is to succeed ; their greatest weakness, their only absurdity, is to be outdone. Philippe de Commines sums up their ethics in a maxim : ' Ceulx qui gaignent,' says he, ' en ont tousjours l'honneur.'

Patelin scored an immense success. It had two sequels, both worthless, and was often quoted. If that merry friar Guillaume Alexis is not the first to allude, by citation, to our farce, the earliest known record of it may be found in a legal document. This document, a grant of pardon issued by Louis XI before Easter, 1469, recites that one Jean de Costes, who had been employed in the King's chancellery, was drinking one day with several companions at an inn kept by Glaude Sillon at Tours. After supper Jean de Costes stretched himself out on a bench by the fire, saying, 'By God, I am ill!'; and, as the document tells us, he addressed these words to the wife of the aforesaid Glaude Sillon and said, ' I would fain sleep here, and not go back to-day to my lodgings.' Hereupon the aforesaid Le Danceur [who seems to have started the quarrel in which he was killed] went and spoke to the aforesaid suppliant as follows: 'Jehan de Costes, I know you well; you fancy to play Patelin and to feign illness, because you are planning to sleep here' (*Jehan de Costes, je vous cognoys bien: vous cuidez pateliner et faire du malade, pour cuider coucher ceans*).

In a short time the name Patelin had become proverbial and the *Farce of Patelin* had attained a vogue unparalleled in the history of the early stage and rarely equalled since. Of five editions printed between 1485, or thereabouts, and 1500, five unique exemplars are known to survive; several other editions must have existed. Two or three editions published shortly after 1500 are also represented by only one exemplar; at least a score appeared during the sixteenth century, and the popularity of our farce scarcely waned till French playwrights began, as we have seen, to be ashamed of what had once delighted the common folk, and set learnedly about imitating Roman comedy; but the *esprit gaulois* could not be quelled, and

[xxxi]

we find it once more, more vigorous than ever and lifted out of its wallow of lubricity, though not yet angelically pure, in the comedies of Molière.

Patelin is not the starting-point of any school, but it would be a long task to narrate the history of its influence on literature in and out of France. Some of its phrases are used by Guillaume Alexis, Coquillart, and others. In 1560 Estienne Pasquier, having read and reread this 'sample' of the old farces, declared it equal to any Greek, Latin, or Italian comedy. Marot had no doubt read it, and Rabelais quotes it again and again. He speaks of the 'noble Patelin,' who was evidently a rascal after his own heart, and we may be sure that Rabelais's famous scene between Panurge and Pantagruel was inspired by *Patelin*. 'Epistemon said, "Parlez vous christian, mon ami, ou langaige patelinois?"' (II, 9.)

It was not Rabelais, however, who first carried Patelin's fame across the Channel; for not later than 1535, and probably ten years earlier, *A Hundred Mery Tales and Quicke Answers* contained an anecdote 'Of hym that payde his dette with crienge bea.' * In 1700 a dull dramatist named Brueys composed, or, to speak more descriptively, he manufactured his *Patelin, comédie, composée en trois actes, avec un prologue, et trois intermèdes,*

* See Notes on the Text, Note xxxv.

[xxxii]

meslés de déclamations, de chants et de danses : Et
representée pour la première fois sans Prologue &
sans intermèdes le 4. Juin 1706.*

Had Monsieur de Brueys been born a humorist,
he would either have written better comedies, or
none. With Palaprat's assistance, the abbé pleased
for a while ; that is the best that can be said for
him. Brueys and his contemporaries liked literary
monsters. They borrowed and muddled, very
much as the compilers of mysteries had done
in the Middle Ages. Unfailingly commonplace,
Brueys tells his readers that he had culled from the
old farce as one might gather gold from a dung-
hill. We need not wonder that the abbé decor-
ated his comedy with a Prologue wherein some
worn-out deities air his theories of the drama. Yet
Brueys's hybrid succeeded, and gave birth in its
turn, *contra naturam*, to *The Village Lawyer*, the
second version of *Patelin* to be made in England.

This curtain-raiser, ascribed without evidence
to the elder Macready,† was performed at The
Haymarket in 1787. *The Village Lawyer*, whose
hero is called not Patelin but Scout, was printed

---

* See *L'Avocat Patelin*. Translated by S. F. G. Whitaker,
London, 1905 ; reviewed in *The Evening Post*, New York,
June 12, 1905, and in *The Athenæum*, London, August 26,
1905.

† See the *Dictionary of National Biography*, vol. xxxv, p. 277.

at Dublin in 1792, having been received, so the title-page declares, with ' Universal Applause ' in London and in Dublin.

Was this little piece published, without regard for its author, from one of those unsigned manuscripts which actors use ? Or is it possible that the author had a scrupulous conscience ? Whatever the truth may be, *The Village Lawyer* is by no means so absurd as Brueys's hotchpotch of modernised medieval folk and pseudo-antique divinities.

The Village Lawyer was performed at the Park Theatre, in New York City, in November, 1801, and again in 1808. The elder Jefferson (1774–1832)* played the part of Sheepface, who is merely Thibaut Agnelet (or ' Lambkin '), in his second reincarnation. In 1863 one James Maffitt, a pirate by nature, but a playwright by trade, on some marauding voyage, fell upon *The Village Lawyer*. Mrs. Scout and her daughter Kate, being no longer useful, were made to walk the plank. Scout, known in other days as Master Pierre Patelin, or Lawyer Patelin, became Benjamin Hardcrust. Maffitt was thus rid of any necessity of seeing Kate wedded to Charles, the son of

* Jefferson left England about 1795. Probably he included *The Village Lawyer* in his repertory because it was still popular.

[xxxiv]

Snarl (Brueys's Guillaume), and he needed no more than a week or so to shear the legal episode out of *The Village Lawyer.*

*The Mutton Trial,** for thus Maffitt named his plagiary, was performed by four members of a troop of minstrels, at the American Theatre, a New York playhouse, in 1863. The cast of characters was as follows:

SHEEPFACE, a Shepherd	*Charles White*
BENJ. HARDCRUST, a Lawyer . .	*Nelse Seymour*
OLD SNARL, a Farmer	*Billy Burke*
JUSTICE	*James Wambold*

These four actors were probably blackened to look like negroes, and perhaps they remained so throughout the long and varied performance in which *The Mutton Trial* was but an interlude lasting 'twenty minutes.' That they imitated negro manners or negro speech is inconceivable.

A notion as to the quality of Maffitt's style may

* *The Mutton Trial* | *An Ethiopian Sketch, in Two Scenes* | *By James Maffitt* | *Arranged by Charles White* | *The Celebrated Ethiopian Comedian* | *Author of* | *Magic Penny* | *Jolly Millers* [here follows a list of two score pieces] etc., etc. | *As first Produced at the American Theatre, No. 444 Broadway* | *New York* | etc., etc. A copy of this rare farce, whose existence was made known to me by Mr. Brander Matthews, is preserved at the Library of Congress, where it was deposited to obtain copyright in 1874.

be derived from the following citations. 'Well,' says Hardcrust, 'here I am, Lawyer Hardcrust, with scarcely enough money in my clothes to buy a meal of victuals.' And on advising Sheepface how to outwit the law, Hardcrust speaks as follows: 'Well, now understand my plan. Any question asked you by the Judge, the Court (*sic*), or the jury (*sic*), you must answer it in the language of the old ewes when they call their young.' As in *The Village Lawyer*, Sheepface responds, 'That is my mother tongue.' In *The Village Lawyer*, when Scout attempts to collect his fee but gets nothing save *baa!*, he cries out angrily, 'What, again! braved by a Mongril Cur, a bleating Bellweather, a — '; in the American piece Hardcrust exclaims, 'What! am I to be outwitted by a country wetherbull!' Further examples from Maffitt's plagiary would only serve to show that the original Patelin, cheapened by Brueys, and afterwards by an unknown British hack, fell almost to the level of a buffoon, on his third and final reincarnation.

To retell a long story in few words, the farce of *Patelin* came into being in France before 1469, and assuredly it owes nothing to the story of Mak, the Thief in what is called 'The Shepherds' Play,' in the *Towneley Mysteries*; its origin is lost in the same darkness as envelops its author. *Patelin* is wholly French and wholly medieval; it alludes to nothing 'classic,' and has nothing whatever to do with ancient comedy. Its popularity was immense; by 1520 it had been freely translated into Latin by Connibert; by 1535 it was known in England (perhaps, too, in Germany); about 1787 some nameless British playwright borrowed or stole from Brueys's hotchpotch (1700) all the plot and many details of *The Village Lawyer*; about 1863 James Maffitt plundered *The Village Lawyer* and called his booty *The Mutton Trial*; this final version of *Patelin* was performed by 'Ethiopian' minstrels in New York City, some four centuries after the original farce had first appeared in France.

No other farce written in the Middle Ages, and naturally no later comedy, can claim so long and varied a history; yet in a mere sketch not half that history can be told, but the popularity of this farce is no puzzle: its author hit upon an extraordinarily clever plot,* and, unlike his contemporaries,

---

* This plot, like most others, was doubtless not 'created.' As early as 1370, or thereabouts, Eustache Deschamps had composed the so-called *Farce de Mestre Trubert*, a dramatic satire aimed at pettifoggers, or, one might say, at lawyers in general; for the Bar was in ill repute throughout the Middle Ages.

Trubert is hoodwinked by his client Entroignart (= Cheatem), who asks his advice about the theft of an almond, a trifling fact that had led to serious consequences. Having got his retainer, Trubert, not altogether unlike Patelin, proceeds to enumer-

he had the genius to tell his fable dramatically in charming verse. Like a precocious child that has aroused laughter by some show of wit, he repeats his jests until they begin to stale; but his insight is keen, and his characters are drawn so firmly that each is a type, possible in nature, but nowhere else to be found in literature. Although close examination reveals more than one inconsistency, the illusion that he creates betokens a rare imaginative power, a clear vision, and so objective a portrayal of that vision that the author nowhere gives a genuine clue as to his own personality. We may agree with Renan in thinking the author of *Patelin* a low and heartless jester; but he betrays nothing, except, perhaps, a tendency to delight us with humour wantonly cruel; he is not a moraliser but a dramatist, and the best dramas are surely those that seem to tell the most about other men and the least about their authors.

ate some of the many wiles by which he knows how to evade the law. He then suggests a game of dice which results in his losing his money and his clothes. Similar stories about the Bar were popular, and it is likely that the author of *Patelin*, perhaps himself a lawyer, built his legal episode on a like anecdote, and that he welded it to the story of some scalawag who had cheated a creditor by shamming illness or insanity, a frequent occurrence in real life. See vol. VII, pp. 155–174, and vol. XI, pp. 293 and 294, of the works of Deschamps, in the edition published by the Société des Anciens Textes français.

THE FARCE OF

MASTER PIERRE PATELIN

Master Pierre Patelin

PATELIN, GUILLEMETTE

Master Pierre begins

BY Saint Mary! Guillemette, for all my pains to pick up something, or bag a little pelf, not a penny can we save. Now, I have seen the time when I had clients.

Guillemette

Aye, true enough! I was thinking of the tune your lawfolk are warbling. No, you are not thought so able by any manner of means as you used to be. I 've seen the day when everybody must have you to win his suit; now you 're called everywhere the Briefless Barrister.

Patelin [*as if he had not heard*]

Again, I don't say it to brag, but in the circuit where we hold our sessions there's no one abler, except the Mayor.

Guillemette [*naïvely*]

Aye, but he has read the Conjuring-book, and he studied a great while to be a scholar.

Patelin

Whose case ever lags, if I set hand to it? And yet I never learnt my letters, save a little, but I'll venture to say that I can chant by the book with our priest as well as if I'd been as long in school as Charlemaine in Spain!

Guillemette

What is that worth to us? Not a rap! We're all but starved; our clothes are downright sieves, and there's no telling where new ones are to come from. Ha! a fig for all you know!

Patelin

Tush, tush! Upon my conscience, if I care to set my wits at work, I shall find a way to get some finery. Please God, we shall see better days and be up again in no time. Oh, God's deed is done with speed. If it behooves me to stick to business, they 'll not be able to find my peer.

Guillemette

Aye, that they will not! At cheating you 're a masterhand.

Patelin

At regular law! by the Lord who made me!

Guillemette

Upon my word, at gulling, you mean. Oh, I know what I am talking about; for, to tell the truth, though you 've neither education nor common sense, you are reckoned about the greatest slyboots in the whole parish.

Patelin

Nobody is so good at handling cases.

Guillemette

Heaven save me! You mean at plucking gulls. They say so anyhow.

Patelin

So they do of those who sport their silks and satins, and talk of being barristers; but they 're not! Enough of this prattle: I 'm going to market.

[5]

Guillemette [*astonished*]

To market?

Patelin [*mimicking her*]

Yes, to market, my gentle pricer. Now, what if I buy a strip of cloth, or some other trifle for household use ? . . . Our clothes are nothing but rags.

Guillemette

You have n't a copper. What can you do there ?

Patelin [*laying his forefinger on his nose and winking craftily*]

That 's telling ! If I fail, my dear, to fetch you cloth enough for both of us, and to spare, then I 'm a fibber ! [*Playfully surveying Guillemette.*] What colour suits you best ? A greenish grey ? Or Brussels cloth ? Or some other sort ? Tell me that.

Guillemette

Whatever you can get. Borrowers must not be choosers.

Patelin [*counting on his fingers*]

For you, two ells and a half, and for me, three, or rather, four. That makes . . .

Maistre pierre commence

Saincte marie, guillemette
Pour quelque paine que ie mette
Acabasser na ramasser
nous ne pouons rien amasser
or Biz ie que iauocassoye

Patelin, counting on his fingers

Guillemette

Who the mischief will trust you with this cloth? You are counting your chickens before they 're hatched.

Patelin

What do you care? They 'll trust me, beyond a doubt, — and be paid on Doomsday; for it won't be sooner.

Guillemette

Go along, my lamb; by now somebody else may have it on.

Patelin [*almost to himself, as he walks slowly away*]

I will buy either grey or green, and for an undergarment, Guillemette, I want three quarters, or a whole ell of fine dark goods.

Guillemette [*shaking her head*]

God help me! so you do. Be off with you! [*Calling, as he disappears.*] And don't forget your dram, if you can come by it for nothing!

Patelin

Take care of everything!   [*Exit.*]

[8]

Guillemette [*giving vent to her excitement with an exclamation half oath, half sigh*]

What merchant . . . ? [*Brightening*.] If he only might be stark blind !

SCENE II

(*At the shop of Guillaume Joceaulme, Draper*)

PATELIN, THE DRAPER

Patelin [*peering into the Draper's shop*]

Not there? . . . I have my doubts. . . . Aye, by Saint Mary, so he is. He 's fussing with his goods. [*While Patelin is reconnoitring, the Draper emerges and lays several rolls of goods on his counter. Then, on looking up, he spies the Lawyer, who greets him with a beguiling smile.*] My worthy sir, God bless you !

Guillaume Joceaulme, Draper

And give you joy !

Patelin [*leaning his hands on the counter*]

I have been really longing to see you, Guillaume. How is your health? You 're feeling tiptop, eh?

[9]

The Draper

Aye, that I am!

Patelin [*holding out his hand*]

Here! your fist! How goes it with you?

The Draper

Why, first rate, really — and yours to command.
. . . . And how are you?

Patelin [*giving the Draper a friendly clap on the shoulder*]

By the Apostle Saint Peter, your humble servant is as happy as a lark . . . So you're feeling
merry, eh?

The Draper

To be sure. But merchants, you must know,
can't always have their way.

Patelin

How is business? It yields enough, I trust, to
keep the pot a-boiling?

The Draper

Afore Heaven, my good sir, I scarcely know.
[*Imitating the cluck of a driver to his horse.*] It's
always gee up! go along! [*He sighs.*]

[10]

Patelin [*in a reminiscent revery*]

Ah, he was a knowing man! — your father was, I mean. God rest his soul! [*Scanning the Draper with amazement.*] When I look at you, I can't believe I'm not looking at him! What a good merchant he was! and clever? . . . [*Waving his hand in such a way as to suggest the almost limitless ability of the elder Joceaulme.*] I swear, your face is as like his as a regular painting. . . . If God ever took pity on any being, may he grant your father his soul's pardon! [*Takes off his hat and glances piously toward heaven. The Draper follows suit.*]

The Draper [*sanctimoniously*]

Amen! Through his mercy! And ours, too, when it shall please him! [*Both replace their hats.*]

Patelin [*with a touch of melancholy*]

My faith! Many a time and most copiously he foretold me the days that we are come to. Again and again the memory has come back to me. [*After a slight pause.*] Then, too, he was deemed one of the good . . .

The Draper [*interrupting Patelin's reminiscences by offering him a seat*]

Do sit down, sir. It's high time I asked you to [*self-reproachful*], but it was just like me to forget.

[11]

*Patelin [as if anything concerning his own welfare
were of no importance]*

Tut, tut, man! I'm comfortable. . . . He used
to . . . [*Another interruption by the Draper, who,
in his zeal to show good manners to a prospective
customer, leans over his counter as far as he can,
grasps Patelin by the shoulders, and endeavours to
force him to sit down.*]

The Draper

Now, really you must be seated.

Patelin [yielding]

Gladly. [*A short pause, after which Patelin
blithely resumes his yarn.*] Oh, you shall see what
wonders he told me! . . . I'll take my oath! in
ears, nose, mouth, eyes, — no child was ever so
like his father. [*Pointing.*] That dimpled chin!
Why, it's you to a dot! And if anybody told
your mother that you were not your father's son,
he'd be hard up for a quarrel. I really cannot
imagine how ever Nature among her works made
two so similar faces. Each marked like the other!
Why look! If you had both been spat against a
wall in the self-same manner and in one array, you
wouldn't differ by a hair. But, sir, good Laurentia,
your step-aunt, is she still living?

[12]

The Draper [*mystified*]

Of course she is.

Patelin [*rising*]

How comely she seemed to me, and tall, and straight, and full of graces ! . . . Od's dear mother ! you take after her in figure, as if they had copied her in snow. No family hereabouts, I think, comes up to yours for likenesses. The more I see you, . . . Bless my soul ! [*Pointing to a mirror.*] Look at yourself. You're looking at your father ! [*Clapping Joceaulme on the back with jovial familiarity.*] You resemble him closer than a drop of water, I'll be bound ! . . . What a mettlesome blade he was ! the worthy man, — and entrusted his wares to whoever wished them. Heaven forgive him ! He always used to laugh so heartily with me. Would to God the worst man in the world resembled him ! There'd be no robbery or stealing, as there is. [*Feeling a piece of cloth.*] How well made this cloth is ! how smooth it is, and soft, and nicely fashioned !

The Draper [*proudly*]

I had it made to order from the wool of my own flock.

Patelin [*overflowing with admiration*]

You don't say so ! What a manager you are !

[13]

[*Jocularly.*] It's the pater all over again. Blood
will tell! . . . [*Awestruck.*] You are always,
always busy.

The Draper [*solemnly*]

Why not? To live, a body must be careful and
put up with trials. [*He looks at Patelin, who nods
assent.*]

Patelin [*handling another piece of goods*]

Was this one dyed in the wool? It's as strong
as Cordovan leather.

The Draper [*showing off the weave of his goods*]

That is good cloth of Rouen make, and well
fulled, I promise you.

Patelin

Now, upon my word, that's caught me; for I
had no thought of getting cloth, when I came; by
George, I had n't. I 'd laid aside some four score
crowns for an investment; but twenty or thirty of
them will fall to you; I see that plainly, for the
colour is so pleasing it gives me an ache. [*Sighs,
as if feeling a rapture akin to pain.*]

The Draper [*eagerly*]

Crowns, you say? Now can it be that your
borrowers would take an odd sum?

[14]

Pathelin

Dea ceſt trop

Le drappier

ha Bous neſcaues
comment le drap eſt encheri
treſtout le Beſtail eſt peri
ceſt yuer par la grant froidure

It's too much!

Patelin

Why, yes, if I chose. It 's no odds to me what sort of money 's paid. [*Picking up the cloth again.*] What kind of goods is this? . . . Really, the more I see it, the worse I dote. I must have a coat of that, — to be brief, — and another for my wife, as well.

The Draper

Cloth costs like holy oil. You shall have some, if you like. Ten or twenty francs are sunk so quickly!

Patelin

I don't care: give me my money's worth. [*Whispering in the Draper's ear.*] I know of another coin or two that nobody ever got a smell of.

The Draper

Now you 're talking! That would be capital!

Patelin

In a word, I 'm hot for this piece, and have some I must.

The Draper

Well then, first you must make up your mind how much you want. To begin with, though you had n't a brass farthing, the whole pile is at your service.

[16]

Patelin [*gazing rather absent-mindedly at the cloth*]
I know that well, thank you.

The Draper
You might like some of this sky-coloured
stuff?

Patelin
First, how much is a single ell to cost? [*On
saying this, Patelin holds up a penny so that the
Draper may get a good look at it.*] Here is a penny
to seal the bargain in God's name; God's share
shall be paid first: that stands to reason, and let
us do nothing without calling him to witness.
[*Piously doffs his hat, strides solemnly to a box set up
in the market-place for receiving God's pennies, drops
the coin in, and returns to the Draper.*]

The Draper
Upon my word, you speak like a g o o d man,
and I'm glad to hear you. Shall I set the very
lowest price?

Patelin
Yes.

The Draper [*decisively*]
It will cost you four and twenty pence an ell.

Patelin
Go to! Four and twenty pence!
Heaven save the mark!

The Draper [*laying his hand on his heart*]

By this soul! it cost me every whit of that, and I must lose nothing by the sale.

Patelin

E x c u s e m e! it's too much.

The Draper

You'd never believe how cloth has risen! This winter the live-stock all perished in the great frost.

Patelin

T w e n t y pence! t w e n t y pence!

The Draper

And I swear I will have my price. Wait till Saturday and you shall see what it's worth. Wool on the fleece, of which there used to be a plenty, cost me on Saint Maudeleyne's day eight good blanks, — my oath on it, — for wool I once got for half as much.

Patelin

Od's blood! Then I will buy, without further haggling. Come, measure off!

The Draper

And pray how much must you have?

[18]

Patelin

That is easy to answer. What is the width?

The Draper

Brussels width.

Patelin [*as if to himself, and cocking his head without looking at the Draper. On saying ' she's tall,' he makes a gesture as if he were laying his hand on the head of an imaginary Guillemette*]

For m e, three ells, and for h e r (she's tall), two and a half. In all, six ells . . . Why, no it is n't! What a dunce I am!

The Draper

There wants but half an ell to make the six.

Patelin

Give me the even six, then. I need a hat as well.

The Draper [*pointing to the other end of his strip of cloth*]

Take hold there. We'll measure. Here they are, and no scrimping. [*He measures.*] One, . . . and two, . . . and three, . . . and four, . . . and five, . . . and six!

[19]

Patelin

Saint Peter's paunch! Measured fair and square!

The Draper [looking at Patelin, then turning his ell in the other direction. Naïvely]

Shall I measure back again?

Patelin [with cheerful disdain]

Oh, h—— no! In selling goods there's always a little gain or loss. How much does it all amount to?

The Draper

Let us see. At four and twenty pence, each, — for the six ells, nine francs.

Patelin [aside]

Hm! Here goes! [*To the Draper.*] Six crowns?

The Draper

So help me! Yes.

Patelin

Now, sir, will you trust me for them? . . until anon, when you come? [*The Draper shows symptoms of suspicion.*] Nay, 'trust' is not the word, for you shall get your crowns at my door, in gold, or, if you like, in change.

The Draper [*ungraciously*]

Oh thunder! that's off my road.

Patelin [*with playful irony*]

By my lord Saint Giles, now you're telling gospel truth! Off your road! That's it! You are never ready to drink at my house, but this is the time you shall.

The Draper

Good Lord! I scarcely do anything but drink! [*After a moment's hesitation.*] I'll come, but let me tell you it's bad policy to give credit on a first sale.

Patelin

What if I pay for it, not in silver or copper, but in good yellow coin? [*Craftily.*] Oho! and you must have a bite of that goose my wife is roasting!

The Draper [*aside*]

The man drives me mad. [*Aloud.*] Go on! Away! I will follow you then, and bring the cloth.

Patelin [*nimbly seizing the bundle of goods*]

Nothing of the sort! How will it burden me? Not a whit, beneath my elbow . . so.

The Draper [*trying to recover his property*]

No, indeed, sir! it would look better for me to bring it.

Patelin [*tucking the cloth into his long gown*]

I'll be hanged if you go to such pains! See how snug it lies, here, under my elbow. What a jolly hump it will give me! Ah! now it's all right! [*With mock hilarity.*] We'll have a fling before you leave.

The Draper

I beg you, hand over my money as soon as I've arrived.

Patelin

I will that, and by gracious I'll see to it you eat heartily. I'd be sorry to have anything about me to pay with now. [*Very archly.*] At least you will come and try my wine. When your late father went by my house he used to sing out, 'Hullo, old pal!', or, 'What's the good word?', or, 'How do you do?' But you don't care a straw for poor folk, you rich men!

The Draper [*flattered but deprecatory*]

Oh, now, I say! it's we who are poorer . . .

Patelin [*laughing incredulously*]

Whew! Well, good-bye, good-bye! Turn up soon where I told you, and we 'll have a good drink, you can count on that.

The Draper

I 'll do so. Go ahead, then, and see that I get gold! [*Patelin starts homeward.*]

SCENE III

(*In the market-place*)

Patelin

Gold! To think of it! Gold! The devil! I hit the nail on the head that time! [*Overcome by a sense of immense absurdity.*] No! gold! I 'd see him hanged. [*Chuckling.*] Pshaw! He sold to me not at my price, but at his own ; he shall be paid, however, at mine. He must have gold ; he shall get it — in the sweet bye and bye! Would he might run without stopping till he is paid! By Saint John, he 'd travel further than from here to Pampeluna! [*Enters an alley and disappears.*]

[23]

SCENE IV

(At the Draper's shop)

The Draper.

Those crowns he's going to pay me sha'n't get a peep at sun or moon this year, unless they're stolen from me. It takes two to make a bargain. That trickster is a big gull to buy at four and twenty pence an ell cloth not worth twenty !

SCENE V

(At Patelin's. Guillemette is sitting near the window and facing it, so as to get all the light that enters through its small and somewhat murky panes. On her lap lies a garment which she is patching. Presently the door is softly opened and Patelin looks in. Seeing that Guillemette's back is turned, and that she is unaware of his presence, he steals toward her, grinning as he thinks what a surprise she is about to get. Suddenly, when he is quite close, she hears him and turns round with a start. Then Patelin begins to speak, archly and in a tone of triumph.

PATELIN, GUILLEMETTE

[24]

Patelin

Have I some?

Guillemette [*startlea*]

Some what?

Patelin

What ever became of that old gown of yours?

Guillemette

Much need there is of telling! What will you
do with it?

Patelin

Nothing! nothing! Have I some? . . . .
I told you so! Is this the cloth? [*He whips the
roll of goods from under his gown and flaunts it in
the face of the astounded Guillemette.*]

Guillemette

Holy Mother! Now, as I hope to live, whose
chest did that come from? [*A little frightened.*]
Heaven! what scrape have we got into now?
Dear! dear! and who's to pay for it?

Patelin

Who, you ask? By Saint John, it's paid for.

[25]

The chap who sold me that is n't crazy, my pet, oh, no! May I be hanged by the neck if he's not well fleeced. The rascally curmudgeon has caught it across the bum.

Guillemette

But how much is it to cost?

Patelin

Cost? Nothing! it's paid for. No need of fretting over that.

Guillemette

Paid for? How? You had n't a farthing.

Patelin

Oh yes, I had. I had a penny.

Guillemette [*ironically*]

Oh, very fine! Fie! You swore to pay, or you gave a note of hand. That is how you came by it! And when the note falls due they'll come and seize our things and carry off everything we own.

Patelin [*reassuringly*]

Upon my word, I gave but a penny for it all.

Guillemette

Benedicité Maria! A penny? Impossible!

[26]

Patelin [*leaning toward her*]

You may pluck out this eye, if he got more, or if he gets more, bawl though he may.

Guillemette

But who is he, anyhow?

Patelin

A numbskull called Guillaume, whose surname is Joceaulme; since you must know.

Guillemette

But how came you to get it for a penny? What was your game?

Patelin

It was for God's-penny; and yet, had I said, 'Let's bind the bargain with a drink,' I'd have kept my penny. Anyhow, 'twas well worked. God and he shall share that penny, if they care to; for it is all they shall get, no matter how they carry on.

Guillemette

How came he to trust you? he's such a surly customer.

Patelin

Dash me if I did n't make him out such a noble lord that he almost gave it me. I told him what

[27]

a jewel his late father was. 'Ah, brother,' says I, 'what good stock you come of! No family hereabouts,' says I, 'compares with yours for virtues,' but drat me! what riff-raff! The most ill-tempered rabble, I suppose, in all this kingdom. 'Guillaume, my friend,' says I, 'what a likeness you do bear your good father! and in every feature!' God wot how I heaped it on! And meanwhile I interlarded something about woollens. 'And then,' says I, 'heavens! how kind he was about trusting folks with his wares! and so meekly! You're he,' says I, 'his spitten image!' Yet you might have hauled the teeth out of that rascally old porpoise, his late father, or his monkey of a son, before they'd trust a fellow with as much as that! [*snaps his fingers*] or even be polite. Anyhow, I made such an ado and talked so much that he trusted me with six ells.

Guillemette

Yes, and he'll never get them back.

Patelin [*derisively*]

Get them back? He'll get the devil back!

Guillemette [*suggesting by mimicry the action in the fable of the Fox and the Crow*]

I call to mind the fable of the Crow that had

[28]

perched on a cross, some ten or twelve yards high. In his beak he was holding a cheese. A Fox strolled along that way and spied the cheese. Thought he to himself, 'Now, how am I going to get it?' Then he stood beneath the Crow. 'Ah,' says he, 'how handsome you are! and your song is so full of melody!' The Crow, like a fool, hearing such praises of his voice, opened his beak to sing. Down dropped the cheese, and in a trice Master Renard had it tight between his teeth and off he went! That, I'll wager, is what happened to this cloth. You wheedled him out of it, just as Renard got the cheese.

Patelin

He is coming to eat some goose, — on a wild goose chase, I mean. Now here's our game. Of course he will be braying to get money on the spot; so I've hatched out a nice arrangement. I'll simply lie on my bed, and play sick; then, when he comes, you will say, 'Oh, do speak low!' Then you must groan and pull a long face. 'Alas!' (you'll say) 'he fell sick these two months past,' — or say six weeks, — and if he cries, 'That's all flim-flam, for he has just been at my shop,' you must say, 'Alas! this is no time to romp!' Then let me pipe him a little tune, for music is all he shall get.

[29]

Guillemette

Trust me to play the game, — but if you slip up again, you may smart for it : I bet you 'll catch it a good bit worse than the other time.

Patelin

Hush now ! I know what I 'm about. We must both do as I say.

Guillemette

For goodness sake remember that Saturday they put you in the stocks ! You know how every one jeered at you for your trickery.

Patelin

Do stop your chatter : he 'll be here before we know it. That cloth must stay with us [*hiding it under the mattress*]. Now I 'm going to bed.

Guillemette [*laughing at his burlesque preparations*]
Go ahead !

Patelin [*under the bedclothes*]
No laughing, now !

Guillemette [*as she draws the bedcurtains together*]
Well, rather not ! I 'll shed hot tears.

[30]

Patelin

We must stand fast, now. No flinching, or he'll see what's up.

SCENE VI

(*At the Draper's shop*)

The Draper

I must have a parting drink. Why no, I won't! for, by Saint Mat., I shall have some wine with Master Pierre Patelin, and a bit of his goose. And there I'm to receive some funds. I'm in for some plum, there, at the very least, and at no expense! There is no use in staying here; for I can make no further sales. [*Leaves his shop; knocks on Patelin's door.*] Hello! Master Pierre!

SCENE VII

(*At Patelin's*)

THE DRAPER, GUILLEMETTE, PATELIN

[31]

Guillemette [*opening the door a chink and laying her finger on her lips*]

Oh, sir, if you have anything to say, for mercy's sake speak lower!

The Draper

God keep you, mis'ess!

Guillemette

Oh, not so loud!

The Draper [*astonished and puzzled*]

Huh? What is the matter?

Guillemette [*feigning amazement*]

Bless my soul!

The Draper

Where is he?

Guillemette

Alas! Where should he be?

The Draper

The . . . Who?

Guillemette

Ah, sir, how unkind! Where is he? May God in his mercy know! He has lain on the very same spot, poor martyr, without budging, for e l e v e n weeks.

[32]

Guillemette

Helas sire
pour dieu se bous boules rien dire
parles plus bas
        Le drappier
Dieu bous gart dame
           Guillemette
Ho, plus bas

The Draper visits Patelin

The Draper [*staring open-mouthed*]

Who's this?

Guillemette [*whispering in the Draper's ear*]

Excuse me: I dare not raise my voice. I believe he is resting. He is a little drowsy. Alas! he's so done up, poor man!

The Draper [*in amazement*]

Who?

Guillemette

Master Pierre.

The Draper [*indignantly*]

Whew! And didn't he come to purchase six ells of cloth, right now?

Guillemette

Who? He?

The Draper

He came from my shop not half a quarter of an hour ago. Hurry! I am wasting time. Come! No more fooling! My money!

Guillemette

Oh, no joking! This is no time for jokes.

The Draper [*waving his arms*]

Here! My money! Are you crazy? I want nine francs.

[34]

Guillemette

Oh Guillaume! It's no time for gammon, nor for making light of us. Go along and trifle with your simpletons, if you're out for a lark.

The Draper [*angrily*]

I'll have nine francs, or I'll be damned!

Guillemette [*trying to keep from laughing, while she wipes away imaginary tears*]

Oh dear! sir, not everybody is so fond of laughter and clap-trap as you are.

The Draper [*beseechingly*]

I say; please, no kidding; do fetch me Master Pierre.

Guillemette

Bad luck to you! What? To-day?

The Draper [*gesticulating angrily*]

Isn't this place, here, where I am, in the house of Master Pierre Patelin?

Guillemette

Yes! And may they stick you into bedlam! [*crossing herself*] — but not me! Sh!

[35]

The Draper

The devil and all! [*Waxing sarcastic.*] Have
I no right to ask?

Guillemette [*crossing herself again, as if the devil
might really appear; then laying her fingers on
her lips and glancing mysteriously toward Patelin's hiding-place*]

God bless my soul! Sh! Lower, if you wish
him to stay asleep!

The Draper [*very satirical*]

Lower? How 'lower'? Shall I whisper it
down in your ear? at the bottom of the well? or
of the cellar?

Guillemette

My goodness! What a babbler you are! Anyhow, that is always the way with you.

The Draper [*in petulant protestation*]

Damn it all! Now, let me tell you, if you ex-
pect me to whisper .... [*Angrily.*] Say now! As
for such wrangling, I 'm not used to it. [*Bearing
on each word.*] The truth is that Master Pierre
took six ells of cloth to-day.

Guillemette [*shrilly*]

Huh? Oh, come! T o-d a y? Well, I never!

Look here, now! Took what? . . . Hang me, if it is n't the sober truth! He is in such a plight, poor man, that he has n't left his bed for e l e v e n weeks — I believe you are making sport of us. Now, is there any reason in it? Law now! you clear out of my house! [*Wringing her hands.*] Oh dear! oh dear!

The Draper
You were telling me to speak so low! Holy Mother! you are shrieking!

Guillemette [*almost in a whisper*]
Upon my soul, it is you who are making all the noise!

The Draper
Look here! I must be off. Hand over . . .

Guillemette [*forgetting herself and letting her voice rise to a high key*]
Sh! Speak low, will you!

The Draper
But it 's you who 'll rouse him! Great guns! You talk ten times louder than I do! [*Emphatically.*] I want you to let me go.

Guillemette
Eh? What is this? Are you cracked? or have you been drinking? In heaven's name!

[37]

The Draper

Drinking? My word! There's a pretty question!

Guillemette

Oh dear! Speak lower!

The Draper [*meekly*]

I ask payment for six ells of cloth, lady, — for pity's sake.

Guillemette

It's all in your eye! And who did you give it to?

The Draper

To himself.

Guillemette

Fine trim he's in for buying cloth! Alas! he can't budge [*begins to sob; the Draper thinks hard.*] He's in no need of clothes; never more will he be drest in any garment but a white one, nor leave the spot where he is lying, unless he goes feet first.

The Draper

This must have happened since sunrise, then; for I'm sure I talked with him.

Guillemette [*stopping her ears*]

Your voice is so shrill! Be quiet, for pity's sake!

[38]

The Draper [in a perfect tantrum]

It's you, upon my oath! It's you! Oh, damn it! Od's blood! this is torment. If some one paid me, I would go my way. Afore Heaven! whenever I have trusted, this is what I've always got for it.

SCENE VIII

PATELIN, GUILLEMETTE, THE DRAPER

Patelin [as if he had just awakened]

Guillemette! A little rosewater! Prop me up! Tuck me in behind! Pah! No one's listening. The ewer! A drink! Rub the soles of my feet!

The Draper

I hear him there.

Guillemette

You do.

Patelin [in a nightcap ; peers out between the cur-
tains and shouts to Guillemette]

Ha, wretch! come here! Who told you to open those windows? Come, cover me! Drive these

black men away! Marmara, carimari, carimara!
Away with them! away!

Guillemette [to Patelin]

What's this? How you behave! Are you
beside yourself?

*Patelin [slowly getting out of bed and pointing, as
he does so, toward the rafters. To the Draper]*

Thou canst not see what I perceive. There
is a black monk, f l y i n g. Catch him! Give him
a stole! [*Approaching the Draper, who retreats
backward, he spits like a cat, turning his fingers into
claws and striking as if he were going to scratch the
Draper's eyes out.*] The cat! the cat! [*Pointing,
and seeming to follow the flight of the imaginary
monk.*] Up, up, he goes!

Guillemette

Oh what is this? Ain't you ashamed! La! this
turmoil has upset him.

*Patelin [returns to bed and falls back on his pillow,
exhausted. To Guillemette, who is bending over him]*

Those physicians have killed me with these
hotchpotches they have made me drink. And yet,
to believe them, it's as simple as moulding wax.

Guillemette [*to the Draper*]

Oh! Have a look at him, sir : he's such a sufferer.

The Draper

You don't mean to say he's fallen sick since just now, when he came from market?

Guillemette

From m a r k e t?

The Draper

Aye. By Saint John, I think he was there. [*To Patelin.*] I want my money for the cloth I lent you, Master Pierre.

Patelin [*pretending to take the Draper for a physician*]

Ho, Doctor John! harder than stone : I have . . . . two small lumps, black, round as balls. Shall I take another clyster?

The Draper

Huh? How do I know? What business is it of mine? It's nine francs I want, or six crowns.

Patelin

These three black little pointed things, — I believe you call 'em 'pills.' They have spoilt my

[41]

jaws. For heaven's sake, Doctor John, no more of them! Pah! there is nothing so bitter! They 've made me let go of everything.

The Draper

They have not! by my father's soul! You have n't let go of my nine francs.

Guillemette [*half aside*]

Hang them! these folks who are always meddling. [*'Shooing' the indignant but helpless Draper.*] Away with you, by all the devils! — as God has nothing to do with it.

The Draper

By the Lord who made me, I will have my cloth before I finish, or my nine francs!

Patelin [*to the Draper, still pretending to take him for 'Doctor John'*]

And my water, does it show, perchance, that I am dying? [*To Guillemette.*] Alas, although he stays, let me not die!

Guillemette [*to the Draper*]

Begone! Is n't it wicked to be splitting his ears with your din?

[42]

The Draper [*throwing up both hands*]

May heaven rue the day it runs foul of him!
[*To Patelin.*] Six ells of cloth! Come, now! upon
your honour, is it fair for me to lose them?

Patelin

Had you only been able to thin my . . . . Doctor
John; it's so hard when it comes out at my . . . .
. . . . that I don't know how I keep on living.

The Draper [*shaking his fist*]

I want nine francs in full, I say, or by Saint
Peter . . .

Guillemette

Dear me! how you plague the man! How can
you be so boisterous? You see clearly that he
takes you for a physician. Alas! the poor Christian has had ill luck enough. Eleven weeks
without a break he's been lying there, poor soul!
[*Clasps her hands and looks like the most dismal hypo-
crite; Patelin rolls over, with a groan.*]

The Draper [*half to himself*]

Od's blood! I can't imagine how this mishap
could have befallen him; for he came this very day
and we struck a bargain, — at least, it seemed to
happen so, if I'm not mistaken.

[43]

Guillemette

My good sir, there 's something amiss with your
memory. Really, I think you had better go and
rest a little; for lots of folks might gossip that you
come in here on my account. Go away! The physicians will be on hand presently, and I would n't
have any one suspect some impropriety: I 'm not
that sort.

The Draper

Oh, curse it all! So this is the fix I 'm in.
[*Mopping his brow.*] I 'll be bound! I was still
thinking . . . You have no goose on the fire?

Guillemette

Hark what he asks! Why, sir, that 's no food
for sick folks. Eat your own geese, and don't come
here to play your monkey tricks. I must say, you
make yourself very much at home.

The Draper

Please don't take it amiss, for I verily believed
. . . [*To himself.*] Still . . . by the sacrament . . .
Pshaw! now I am going to find out! [*Walks away
slowly, muttering as he goes.*] I know full well that
I ought to have six ells, all in one piece; but that
woman has clean upset my wits. He took them;
no doubt of it! [*After reflection.*] Nay, he did not.

The devil! it will not tally! I saw him in Death's clutch—or at least he 's shamming death. [*Ponders again.*] Aye, by 'r Lady, he did! There is no doubt of it; he took them and stowed them away beneath his elbow! [*After more reflection.*] No, he did not! It may be I am dreaming; yet, whether I be asleep or awake, it is not like me to give my goods to any man, however friendly he may be with me. I would not have trusted any one. [*Angrily.*] Od's bod! he took them! and by the death . . . [*Reflecting.*] Nay, I have it! He did not! . . Yet what am I coming to? [*Emphatically.*] He has them! [*After a slight pause he waves his arms desperately and bursts out.*] May a pox take both his body and his soul if I know who has got the best or the worst of it, they or myself! I 'm all at sea. [*Exit.*]

SCENE IX

PATELIN, GUILLEMETTE

Patelin [*still in bed; low to Guillemette*]
Is he gone?

Guillemette [*at the door*]
Be still! I 'm listening. He is humming some

little tune or other under his breath. By the way
he mutters, one might suppose he was losing his
mind.

Patelin

Have n't I lain here long enough? [*After a
pause.*] He dropped in so punctually!

Guillemette [*still listening*]

Maybe he will return. [*Patelin starts to rise.*]
Nay! Heaven forbid! Lie still a while. It would
be all up with us if he found you out of bed.

Patelin

He met his match, the distrustful skinflint!
Served him right!

Guillemette [*leaving her post*]

Of all the rank hucksters that ever were baited
he is the gem! Oh, this is what he gets for un-
godly stinginess. [*She titters loudly.*]

Patelin

For heaven's sake, stop laughing! If he came
back he might play the mischief, and, let me tell
you, we have n't seen the last of him.

Guillemette

I declare! Let anybody who can, keep from
laughing; I can't help it! [*Laughs uproariously.*]

[46]

SCENE X

(At the Draper's shop)

The Draper

By the holy light that shines! For all the babblers, that freshwater barrister shall see me again. Pooh! That income some of his cousins or his aunts were going to furnish him! A likely yarn! Now, by Saint Peter, he has my cloth, the false swindler! I gave it him right here. [Starts for Patelin's in a fury.]

SCENE XI

(At Patelin's)

PATELIN, GUILLEMETTE

Guillemette

When I think of the face he made as he looked at you .. [Laughs.] He dunned so fiercely! [Laughs again.]

Patelin

Quit your cackling! God . . . . . . [crosses him-

[47]

self] . . . bless my soul, if some one should over-hear you we might as well decamp: he's such a crusty customer.

SCENE XII

(*Mostly in the market-place*)

The Draper [*with bitter scorn*]

Ha! a boozing pettifogger! [*Sneering.*] A quack who knows but three lessons and three psalms! [*Ironically.*] The rest of us are brainless clowns, forsooth! By gad, no one was ever fitter to be hanged! He has my cloth, or I'll be damned, and he has tricked me with this game! [*Rapping angrily at Patelin's door.*] Ho, there! mis'ess: where are you hiding?

SCENE XIII

(*At Patelin's*)

THE DRAPER, GUILLEMETTE, PATELIN

Guillemette

My word! he's heard me! [*Looking through the keyhole.*] He seems to be going mad.

[48]

Patelin [*in bed; draws the curtains together*]
I 'll make believe I 'm delirious. Let him in.

Guillemette [*opening the door and trying to look
serious*]
How you yell!

The Draper [*entering noisily*]
Ah ha! you are laughing, eh? Here! My
money!

Guillemette

My stars! What do you think I 've got to
laugh about? There is n't an unhappier creature
under the sun. He is passing away. Never did
you hear such a storming, nor frenzy. His mind
is still astray; he raves, he sings, and then he
babbles and mutters in so many languages! He
will not live half an hour. Upon my soul, I laugh
and weep in the same breath.

The Draper

I know nothing about your laughter or your
weeping. To cut it short, I must be paid!

Guillemette

For what? Are you daft? Are you beginning
to rant again?

[49]

The Draper [*haughtily*]

I am not wont to be thus spoken to when I am
selling my cloth. Would you have me believe the
moon is made of green cheese?

Patelin [*standing on his bed, with his head between
the curtains*]

Now then! the Queen of the Gitterns! Quick!
Fetch her here! I know well she has given birth
to four and twenty gitternkins by the abbot of
Ivernaux: I must stand godfather for him.

Guillemette

Alas! Think about God the Father, my dear,
not about gitterns or gitternkins.

The Draper [*aside*]

Ha! What a pair of humbugs! [*Exploding.*]
Quick now! Plank down hard cash for the cloth
you got of me.

Guillemette

La! If you made one mistake, are n't you sat-
isfied?

The Draper [*appealingly*]

Do you know how it is, dear friend? So help
me God! I 'm not aware of a mistake . . . [*In-*

[50]

dignantly.] Come now! Shell out, or be hanged!
[*Whining*.] How do I wrong you if I come here
to ask for what is mine? For by Saint Peter . . .

Guillemette

Alas! How you rack the man! [*Inspired*.] I
see by your looks that you are not sound. [*Scanning him closely*.] As sure as I am a sinner, if I had
help I'd tie you fast, for you've gone stark mad.

The Draper [*desperately*]

Oh dear, oh dear! I am beside myself at not
getting my money.

Guillemette

Oh what witless talk! Cross yourself! Bénédicité! [*Insisting*.] Make the sign of the cross!

The Draper

Damn me if ever I trust anybody with . . .
[*he begins to speak brokenly, hearing noises from the
bed, where Patelin is about to have a fresh frenzy*]
. . . cloth . . . this . . . year . . . Godamercy!
What an invalid!

Patelin [*leaping down from his bed and striding
about, performing, meanwhile, various antics
which the Draper observes with amazement*]

Mere de diou, la coronade, — par fye, y m'en

[51]

voul anar. — Or renague biou, outre mar. Ventre
de diou! zendict gigone, — castuy carible et res
ne done. — Ne carillaine, fuy ta none, — que de
l'argent il ne me sone! If it's ducats, mum is the
word. [*To the Draper.*] Have you understood,
fair coz?

Guillemette [*to the Draper*]

He once had an uncle near Limoges, a brother
of his aunt-in-law. That, I take it, is why he
jabbers in the gibberish of Limousin.

The Draper

Out on you! He stole away with my cloth
under his arm-pit.

Patelin [*taking Guillemette by the hand and starting to lead her away in princely fashion*]

Venez ens, doulce damiselle. [*Pointing to the
Draper.*] Toadspawn! what's it after? [*Haughtily
commanding the Draper to draw back.*] Avaunt,
scullion, avaunt! [*While the Draper stares, Patelin
strides across the room, snatches up an old gown of
Guillemette's, and in very short order gets himself up
as a priest; he then addresses his bewildered visitor
in exclamative or questioning tones.*] Hither! Has-
ten! Devil, come en chelle vielle monkery. Heh!
fault il que ly prestre rie, quant il deust canter se
messe?

Guillemette

Alas! alas! it will soon be time to give him the extreme unction.

The Draper

But how does he happen actually to speak the Picard tongue? Whence comes this foolishness?

Guillemette

His mother was raised in Picardy; so he speaks Picard now.

Patelin [*going toward the Draper*]

Whence comest thou, merry reveler? Wacarme! liefve godeman. Henriey, Henriey, conselapen. [*Takes the Draper's hands and goes dancing about the room, singing.*] Grile, grile, scohehonden, — zilop, zilop, en mon que bonden, — Disticlien unen desen versen, — mat groet festal ou truit den hersen. [*As he gives the astounded Draper a final twirl, Patelin trips himself, falls, and lies on his back with only enough strength left to gasp, but in this posture he soon gets breath to continue his linguistic antics.*] Vuste vuille pour le frimas! [*Kneels as if at a confessional.*] Faictes venir sire Thomas — tantost qui me confessera!

The Draper

What is this? He will keep on all day talking

foreign languages. If he would only give me a security, or my money, I would go.

Guillemette

Bless my soul! . . . Oh, dear me! You are so outlandish. What will you have? How you can be so stubborn passes my understanding.

Patelin [*to the Draper*]

Or cha, Renouart au Tiné! — Bé deá, que ma couille est pelouse! [*The Draper, determined to get his money by hook or by crook, takes hold of Patelin's gown and gives it a pull.*] Les playes dieu! qu'esse qui s'attaque — a men coul? Esse une vaque? — une mousque? ou ung escarbot? [*The Draper retreats, Patelin crouches behind a chair, with only his head visible.*] Bé deá! j'é le mau saint Garbot! — Suis je des foyreux de Baieux?

The Draper

How can he stand the strain of so much talking? [*Witnessing fresh antics.*] Ho! he is losing his wits! But how does he come to speak Norman?

Guillemette

His schoolmaster was a Norman; so in his last hour the memory of it comes back to him. [*Further capers by Patelin.*] He is giving up the ghost!

[54]

The Draper [*in dismay*]

Thunderation! This is the worst raving that ever I ran foul of. [*To Guillemette.*] I never should have thought he was not this day at market!

Guillemette [*astonished*]

You thought so?

The Draper

Yes, hanged if I did n't; but I see that is n't what happened, at all.

Patelin [*listening, as if he heard some noise in the street*]

Sont il ung asne que j'os braire? [*Sputtering, as if another frenzy were coming on.*] Ha oul dandaoul en ravezeie — Orf ha en euf. [*Behind a chair Patelin changes his costume so as to resemble an old hag. Meanwhile Guillemette and the Draper, clinging to each other, await the next occurrence with a horror in one case shammed, in the other real. Hearing a weird sound from behind the chair, Guillemette cries out, with clasped hands.*]

Guillemette

God help you!

[55]

Patelin [*picks up a broom, and with the handle makes cabalistic figures on the floor, draws a circle round the Draper; then sits astride his broom and goes prancing off like a witch, continuing his mutterings*]

Huis oz bezou dronc nos badou — Digaut an tan en hol madou — Maz rehet crux dan holcon — So ol oz merveil il grant nacon — Aluzen archet epysy — Har cals amour ha coureisy.

The Draper

Alas! Blest Heaven! Hearken to it! He is sinking. How he gurgles! [*To Guillemette.*] But what is he sputtering about? How he mutters! Od's bodykin! he mumbles so I cannot catch a word of it. This is not Christian, or any other tongue, apparently.

Guillemette

It's Breton. His grandmother on his father's side came from Brittany. [*Patelin shows signs of exhaustion.*] He is dying! This shows that he needs his last sacraments.

Patelin [*still astride the broom; to the Draper*]

Hé par Gigon, tu te mens. — Vualx te deu, couille de Lorraine! [*Starts to explain the cabalistic figures to the Draper, who retreats in alarm. Pate-*

lin pursues him, whacking the floor and furniture with his broom. Finally, as the Draper, breathless, takes refuge behind a chair, Patelin addresses him in Latin.] Et bona dies sit vobis, — magister amantissime, — pater reverendissime, — quomodo brulis? que nova? — Parisius non sunt ova! — Quid petit ille mercator? — Dicat sibi quod trufator, — ille qui in lecto jacet, — vult ei dare, si placet, — de oca ad comedendum. [*Falls on the floor. The Draper, who has regained some of his courage, helps Guillemette to put Patelin to bed, bolstering him up with pillows. Patelin continues to mutter.*]

Guillemette

Upon my word, he will die a-talking! How he froths! [*To the Draper.*] Do you not mark how he is steaming? [*Casting her eyes aloft.*] Now his human part is going to its heavenly home. [*Hiding her face in her hands.*] Now I shall be left alone, poor and forlorn.

The Draper [*aside*]

It were well for me to go away before he breathes his last. [*To Guillemette.*] I fear he might be loth, at his decease, to tell you any secrets in my presence, though he would in privacy. Pardon; for I take my oath I thought he had got my cloth. Good bye, ma'am; may God forgive me!

[57]

Guillemette [*showing him out*]

Heaven bless you — and his poor mournful wife!

SCENE XIV

(*In the street*)

The Draper

By all the saints! I 'm flummuxed worse than ever. [*After a short pause.*] 'The Devil, in his stead, took my cloth to tempt me! Bénédicité! [*Crosses himself.*] May he leave me in peace! And since the case so stands, I give the cloth in God's name to whosoever took it. [*Reënters his shop.*]

SCENE XV

(*At Patelin's*)

PATELIN, GUILLEMETTE

Patelin [*jumping out of bed and waving his hand after the departing Draper*]

Go along with you! [*To Guillemette*] How do you like me for a teacher? [*Peeping into the street.*]

Crackbrained Neddie is making for home. [*Taps his head significantly.*] Heavens! he has plenty of rooms to let! . . . At night, when he's in bed, he is likely to see spooks.

Guillemette

How he was bamboozled! And did n't I do my part well?

Patelin

Od's bodykin! You're an angel! We've got cloth enough, I think, to have some clothes! [*With this, Patelin pulls the stolen cloth from the bed, where it has lain hidden, wraps one end round his body and flings the whole strip so that it lies unfolded when it reaches Guillemette's feet. She grasps her end and whirls so that she and Patelin are close together when the curtain falls.*]

SCENE XVI
(*At the Draper's shop*)

THE DRAPER
Later, TIBALT LAMBKIN, *a Shepherd*

The Draper

That's the way! Everybody stuffs me with lies. Everybody carries off my goods, and takes

[59]

what he can get. Of all unlucky men I am the
king. The very shepherds cheat me; but mine,
whom I have always treated kindly, shall be sorry
for flouting me! By the blessèd Virgin, he shall
smart for it!

The Shepherd [*appearing unexpectedly from the left
of the market-place; on being seen by his master,
he removes his cap and bows; then begins to speak
with the thick dull drawl of a born yokel*]

God give you a good day, sweet master, and
a good evening!

The Draper

Oho! So it's thou, foul churl. A good fellow
thou art; aye, good for the gallows!

The Shepherd [*resting his crook on the ground and
stopping, about five feet from the Draper*]

I ax your pardon, master, but some one or other
in striped hosen, which were right disorderly, and
he had a rod in his hand, yet no lash on it, said
to me, says he . . yet I remember not at all well
what it may be, to tell the truth. He spoke to
me of you, master, and of some summons or other.
As for me, holy mother! much I know what it's
all about. He muddled me a-talking about ewes
and court in the afternoon. And he raised a great
hullaballoo for you, master . . .

[60]

Le drappier

quoy dea chascun me paist de lobes
chascun men porte mon auoir
et prent ce quil en peust auoir
or suis ie le roy des meschans
mesment les bergiers des champs
me cabusent ores le mien
aqui iay tousiours fait du bien
il ne ma pas pour bien gabbe

The Shepherd comes to explain

The Draper [shaking his fist in the face of Lamb-kin, who cowers against the wall]

If I do not have thee hauled forthwith before the judge, may I be drowned and blasted! Never shalt thou kill one beast, by my oath, but thou remember it! Anyhow, thou shalt pay me for the six ells . . . . I mean for slaughtering my sheep, and the havoc thou hast wrought me these ten years past.

The Shepherd

Don't believe the slanderers, my good master; for, upon my soul . . .

The Draper

And by Gog's bones, before Saturday thou shalt give me back my six ells of wool . . I mean what was taken from my sheep.

The Shepherd

What wool? Ah! master, I believe you are angry over some other thing. By Saint Lupus! master, I fear to speak when I look at you.

The Draper

Leave me in peace! Out of my sight!—if thou art wise. And thou hadst better be on hand.

[62]

The Shepherd

Master, let us agree. For God's sake, don't go to law about it.

The Draper [*waving him off*]

Begone! Thy business is in a pretty pass! [*Yelling and shaking his fist in Lambkin's face.*] Begone! I say. I 'll make no agreement, nor settle anything, save as the judge shall do. [*He drives the Shepherd out.*] Yah! Unless I 'm wary, every one will be swindling me from now on!

The Shepherd

God be wi' you, sir, and give you joy! [*Crossing the market-place; to himself.*] So I must defend myself. [*Knocks at Patelin's door.*] Is any one within?

SCENE XVII

PATELIN, GUILLEMETTE
Later, THE SHEPHERD

Patelin

Hang me, if he is n't coming back!

Guillemette

Nay, he is not; mercy on me! that would be the very worst.

[63]

The Shepherd [*as Patelin comes out*]
God be with you! God bless you!

Patelin

God keep thee! What wilt thou, my good
fellow?

The Shepherd

They will fine me for default unless I appear for
trial. And, if you like, you will come, sweet master, and defend me; for I know nothing. And I
will pay you well, even though I be ill clad.

Patelin

Come hither, now. Speak up! Which art thou?
— plaintiff? or defendant?

The Shepherd

I have business with a dealer — do you understand, sweet master? — whose ewes I have for a
great while led to pasture and watched for him.
Now, sir, upon my word, I saw he paid me scantly.
. . Shall I tell everything?

Patelin

To be sure! A client should hide nothing from
his counsel.

The Shepherd

It is true, sir, beyond denial, that I basted 'em

[64]

on the skull for him, so that time and again they
went into a swoon and fell dead; no matter how
strong and sound they were. And then, lest he
should lay it to me, I gave him to understand that
they died of the scab. 'Ho!' quoth he, 'take the
'scabby one away from the others; off with her!'
'Right willingly!' quoth I; [*leering*] but that was
done otherwise; for, by Saint John! I ate them,
knowing well what they wanted. Well, sir, this
went on so long, and I slaughtered so many, that
he found it out. And when he saw he was being
deceived, — God help me! — he set somebody to
spy; for they hear them bleat very loud, you
understand, when it's going on. So I have been
caught red-handed; I can never deny it. Now I
beseech you — for my part I have money enough
— that we two steal a march on him. I know well
he has the law on his side, but you will find some
loophole, if you try, so as to give him the worst
of it.

Patelin

By your faith, shall you be glad? [*Winsomely.*]
What will you give me if I upset the plaintiff's
case, and you are acquitted?

The Shepherd

I will pay you not in copper, but in fine gold
crowns.

Patelin

Then your case shall be a good one. And were
it twice as bad, so much the better! and the sooner
I shall do for him! As I am going to apply my
wisdom, how you shall hear me spout, when he
has set forth his suit! Come hither! By the holy
precious blood! Art thou crafty enough to understand a trick? What is thy name?

The Shepherd

By Saint Maurus! it is Tibalt Lambkin.

Patelin [*jocularly*]

Lambkin, hast thou filched many a sucking lamb
from thy master?

The Shepherd

My word! it is quite likely I have eaten above
thirty in three years.

Patelin

Ten yearly to pay for dice and candles. [*Aside.*]
I believe I shall let him have it fair! [*Aloud.*] Dost
think he can find any one forthwith to prove his
facts? That is what the case hinges on.

The Shepherd

P r o v e, sir? Blessèd Mary! By all the saints
in Paradise! instead of o n e he'll have a d o z e n
witnesses against me!

[66]

Patelin

That's a bad feature in thy case. [*Slight pause.*]
Here is what I had in mind. I'll feign to know
naught of thee, that I never laid eyes on thee before.

The Shepherd [*in dismay*]

Lord, no! not that!

Patelin

No, then I won't. But here is what you must
do. If you talk, they will trap you every time, and
in such cases confessions are most prejudicial, and
so harmful that it's the devil and all. Here is the
trick! As soon as they call on you for trial, answer nothing but *ba-a-a* [*mimicking a sheep's bleat*],
whatever they say to you. And if they happen to
curse you, saying, ' Ha, stinking fool! a pox on
thee, villain! Art thou flouting the court?' go
ba-a. 'Oh!' I'll say, ' he is half-witted; he thinks
he is talking to his sheep!' But even if they split
their heads with roaring, not another word! Be-
ware!

The Shepherd

I take it to heart, and truly I will be wary, and
I will do it properly, I promise and affirm.

Patelin

Now heed! No flinching! And whatever I say
or do, give me no other answer.

[67]

The Shepherd

I ? By my sacrament ! call me a fool outright
if I utter to-day another word, to you or to any
one, whatsoever they say to me, but only *ba-a*, as
you have taught me.

Patelin

By Saint John ! There is the prank to outwit
your adversary ! [*In a tone between wheedling
and threat.*] But when it is done, pay me a right
good fee.

The Shepherd

Master, if I do not pay as agreed, never trust
me. But I pray, look carefully to my business.

Patelin

By 'r Lady of Boulogne, the Judge must be
holding court; for he always is on hand by six
o'clock, or thereabouts. Now come along with
me, but we will not take the same road.

The Shepherd

Quite so ! [*shrewdly*] they must n't see that
you 're my lawyer.

Patelin [*threateningly*]

By 'r Lady ! Mind your eye, if you don't pay
generously !

[68]

The Shepherd

Why! as agreed, sir; do not doubt it. [*Sets out.*]

Patelin [*alone*]

Oh, well, half a loaf is better than no loaf at all. I shall hook a minnow, anyhow; and if he is lucky, he will give me a crown or so for my pains. [*Follows the Shepherd into the market-place.*]

SCENE XVIII

(*In the market-place*)

(*Enter Judge, followed by a clerk, a score of archers, bailiffs, and loiterers, who range themselves to the right and left of the market-cross, so as to leave an open space before the Judge's seat. The Judge sits down and surveys the crowd*)

THE JUDGE, PATELIN, THE SHEPHERD, *then* THE DRAPER

Patelin [*removes his hat; to the Judge*]

God bless you, sir, and grant you your heart's desire!

The Judge

Welcome, sir! But cover yourself. There! Take a seat.

[69]

Patelin [*hiding in the crowd, to avoid being seen by the Draper, whose breathless approach brings to him the sudden realisation that the Shepherd's adversary is the very person whom he has himself beguiled*]

Oh, I am all right, sir, if you please ; there's more room here.

The Judge [*brusquely*]

If there is business, have done with it, in order that the court may adjourn.

The Draper [*arrives much flurried, just as the Judge has spoken*]

My lawyer is coming, your Worship. He is finishing a little work that he was at, and it would be kind of you to wait for him.

The Judge [*testily*]

Come, come! I have business elsewhere. If the offending party is here, set forth your case at once. Are you not the plaintiff?

The Draper

I am.

The Judge [*casting his eyes about*]

Where is the defendant? Is he present in person?

[70]

Vous feries bien de la tendre
         Le iuge
He dea ie ailleurs a entendre
se vostre partie est presente
deliures vous sans plus datente
et nestes vous pas demandeur
         Le drappier
Si suis

The court scene

The Draper [*pointing at the Shepherd*]

Yes, there he is, keeping mum ; but God knows he has something to think about.

The Judge [*to the Draper*]

Since you are both here, make known your suit.

The Draper

This, then, is what I am bringing an action against him for. Your Worship, the truth is that for the love of God, and out of charity, I reared him in his childhood ; and when I saw that he was strong enough to work in the fields, to cut it short, I made him my shepherd and set him to watching my flock ; but as true as you are sitting there, your Worship, he has wrought such havoc among my ewes and wethers that, no mistaking, he . . .

The Judge [*officious*]

Now listen ! Was n't he in your hire ?

Patelin [*breaking in, ostensibly to show that the Judge has made a good point*]

Aye, that 's it ! For had he kept him for pure sport, without hire . . .

[72]

The Draper [*recognising Patelin, who hides his face behind his hand*]

The devil get me! If it's not you, and no mistake!

The Judge [*to Patelin*]

How is this? You are holding your hand up. Have you a toothache, Master Pierre?

Patelin [*wincing*]

Yes, my teeth are raising such a row that I never felt worse pains. I dare n't lift my head. [*Waving one hand*.] For God's sake, make him proceed!

The Judge [*to the Draper*]

Go on. Finish your charge. Come! Conclude promptly.

The Draper [*aside, and staring at Patelin*]

By the holy rood, 't is he and no other! [*To Patelin.*] It was you I sold six ells of cloth to, Master Pierre!

The Judge [*to Patelin*]

What is he saying about cloth?

Patelin [*to the Judge*]

He's rambling. He means to come to the

point, but he can't find his way to it, for he lacks the training.

The Draper [half choked with indignation]

Hang me if anybody else took my cloth, by the bloody throat!

Patelin [to the Judge]

How the wretched man lugs his inventions in to make out a case! The pig-headed fellow means, of course, that his shepherd had sold the wool that went into the cloth that made my garment, by saying that he is robbing him, and that he stole the wool of his sheep.

The Draper [to Patelin]

Damn me, if you have n't it!

The Judge [to the Draper]

In the devil's name, be still! You are twaddling. Can you not return to the subject, without delaying the court by such drivel?

Patelin [with one hand still on his jaw]

My teeth ache so; yet I must laugh! [*Looking toward the Draper.*] He 's already in such haste that he does n't know where he left off. We must set him right again.

[74]

The Judge [to the Draper]

Come! Let's stick to those sheep! What happened?

The Draper [is about to return to his sheep, when Patelin, by stepping in front of him, diverts his attention; whereupon he shakes his fist at Patelin and at the same time appeals to the Judge]

He took six ells, worth nine francs!

The Judge [bawling]

Are we greenhorns? or tomfools? Where do you think you are?

Patelin [to the Judge]

Od's blood! He takes us for ganders, I suppose! Oh, he looks so very good! but let me advise that his opponent be examined a bit.

The Judge [regaining his composure]

Very true! He is familiar with the man; he must needs know him. [*To the Shepherd.*] Step forward. Speak.

The Shepherd [shambling forward and looking very dull]

Ba-a!

The Judge

Hoity-toity! Here's a mess! What is this *ba-a*? Am I a goat? Speak to me!

The Shepherd

Ba-a!

The Judge

A murrain on you! Ha! Are you flouting us?

Patelin [*to the Judge*]

Believe me, he is crazy, or stupid, or he fancies he's among his sheep.

The Draper [*wildly, to Patelin*]

Damn me if you are not the very man that took it, — my cloth, I mean. [*To the Judge.*] Oh, you can't imagine, sir, by what deceit . . .

The Judge [*threatening*]

Hold your tongue! Are you an idiot? Leave that matter alone, and let's come to the point!

The Draper

True, your Worship; but the circumstance concerns me; yet on my faith I'll not utter another word about it. Another time it may be different. I shall have to swallow it whole. Well, as I was saying, I gave six ells [*the Judge starts*

[76]

up] . . . I mean, my sheep . . . pray, sir, forgive
me . . . this nice master [*Pierre*] . . . my shepherd,
when he ought to have been in the fields . . .
[*Shaking his fist at Patelin and appealing frantically
to the Judge*]. He told me I should have six
crowns in gold, as soon as I came . . . [*as the
Judge threatens*] . . . I mean, three years ago my
shepherd gave me his word that he would watch
over my flock loyally and do me no damage to it,
nor any villainy, and then . . . [*seeing Patelin*]
now he denies me outright both cloth and money.
[*To Patelin*]. Oh, Master Pierre, truly . . [*Catches
a warning frown from the Judge.*] That scoun-
drel robbed me of the wool of my sheep ; and
healthy though they were, he killed them, and
made them die by pounding out their brains . .
[*Again Patelin distracts his attention.*] When he
had tucked my cloth under his arm-pit he hurried
off, saying I should go and get six gold crowns at
his house.

The Judge

There is neither rime nor reason in all your
railing. What does it mean? Now you interlard
one thing, now another. In short, fore God, I can
make neither head nor tail of it. [*To Patelin.*] He
muddles something about cloth and prattles next
of sheep, helter skelter. What can he be driving
at ?

[77]

Patelin

Now, I undertake that he is keeping back the
poor shepherd's wage.

The Draper [to Patelin]

By heaven, you might hold your tongue! My
cloth . . as true as gospel . . I know where my
shoe pinches better than you or any one. Od's
bones, you have it!

The Judge [to the Draper]

What has he?

The Draper

Nothing, sir. [*Again bursts out.*] Upon my
oath, he is the greatest swindler . . [*The Judge
threatens.*] Oh, I 'll be silent about it, if I can,
and not speak of it again, whatever happens.

The Judge

No! But remember! Now finish speedily.

Patelin [to the Judge]

This shepherd cannot answer the charge without counsel; yet he is afraid, or knows not how
to ask for it. If you were willing to order me to
take his case, I would.

[78]

The Judge [ironically]

His case? You'd get cold comfort out of that,
I should imagine. It's hardly worth while.

Patelin

But, honestly, I don't care to make anything out
of it; let it be done for charity! [*Turning toward
the Shepherd.*] Now I'm going to find out from
the poor lad what he will tell me, and whether,
perchance, he may afford me matter for his defence.
He would have a hard time getting out of it, if
nobody came to his rescue. [*To the Shepherd.*]
Come hither, my friend. [*With an utterly vacant
expression the Shepherd slouches forward a step or
two, with his crook in one hand, and his cap in the
other.*] If any one could find . . . dost thou
understand?

The Shepherd

Ba-a!

Patelin [feigning astonishment]

Ba-a? The devil! What ba-a? Zounds! Art
thou crazy? Tell me thy business.

The Shepherd

Ba-a-a!

Patelin

How ba-a? Dost thou hear thy ewes a-bleat-
ing? Mind, it is to thine interest.

The Shepherd

Ba-a !

Patelin [*entreating*]

Now speak ! Say yes, and no. [*Whispering.*] Well done ! Keep it up !

The Shepherd [*softly*]

Ba-a !

Patelin

Louder, or it may cost thee dear.

The Shepherd [*very loud*]

Ba-a-a !

Patelin [*as, with a despairing gesture, he appeals to the Judge*]

The maddest man is he who drives such a born fool into court ! Oh, sir ! send him back to his ewes : he is a fool by nature.

The Draper [*to Patelin*]

A fool, you say ? Saint Saviour of Asturia ! he has more sense than you !

Patelin [*to the Judge*]

Send him away to watch over his flocks, — never to return. Cursed be whoever cites such a lackbrains into court !

[80]

The Draper [*to the Judge*]

And he is to be sent away before I can be heard?

Patelin [*to the Draper*]

So help me! Yes; since he's out of his mind. Why not?

The Draper [*to the Judge*]

Oh now, sir; at least allow me first to have my say. What I have to say is no trumpery, nor scoffing.

The Judge

Vexation is all that comes of having dolts on trial, either male or female. Listen! To cut the matter short, the court will adjourn.

The Draper [*wistfully*]

Shall they go away without ever having to appear again?

The Judge [*gathering up his robe*]

Well, n o w what . .

Patelin [*to the Judge*]

Appear again! You never saw a madder man, neither in his acts nor in his answers. [*Pointing to the Draper.*] And h e is not a whit better. B o t h

[81]

are brainless fools. I 'll be blessed! between them
they have n't a pennyweight of brains!

The Draper [shaking his fist at Patelin]

You carried it off by lying, — that cloth, I
mean, — and without paying for it, Master Pierre.
Fore God, that was the work of no upright man.

Patelin [to the crowd]

Saint Pintle of Rome! If he is n't mad already, he is g o i n g mad.

The Draper [to Patelin]

I know you by your speech, and by your dress.
I am not mad: I am sound enough to know who
does right by me. [*To the Judge.*] I will tell you
the whole matter, my lord; upon my word I will!

Patelin [to the Judge]

Oh, sir! Bid him be still! [*To the Draper.*]
Ain't you ashamed to wrangle so with this poor
shepherd over three or four measly sheep not worth
two buttons! [*To the crowd.*] He makes more
ado . . .

The Draper [storming and shaking his fists]

What sheep? [*With an expression of weariness
and indignation he gives a couple of turns to an*

imaginary crank.] A hurdy-gurdy! Always the same old tune! [*Shaking his finger in Patelin's face.*] It's to yourself I am talking, — to you! and by all that's holy you shall give it back to me!

The Judge

Look you! I am lucky! [*To the crowd.*] He will never stop bawling!

The Draper [*to the Judge*]

I ask him . . .

Patelin [*to the Judge*]

Make him be still! [*To the Draper.*] Oh goodness! Give that song a rest! Suppose he has lammed six or seven, or a d o z e n, and eaten them. He l l's bells! That is hard on you! You've earned more than that while he's been keeping them.

The Draper [*to the Judge*]

Mark, sir! Mark! When I talk to him of cloth, he answers with his shepherd fooleries! [*To Patelin.*] Six ells of cloth that you put under your arm-pit and walked off with — where are they? Do you mean to give them back to me?

Patelin [*to the Judge*]

Oh, sir! Would you have him hanged for six

[83]

or seven sheep? At least, sir, take time to catch your breath. Don't be so harsh to a forlorn shepherd, who's as naked as my nail.

The Draper

A pretty way to change the subject! It was the devil made me sell cloth to such a customer! [*To the Judge.*] Oh now, your Worship, I ask him . . .

The Judge [to the Draper]

I acquit him of your charge and forbid you to proceed. A great honour it is to have a lunatic in court! [*To the Shepherd.*] Away to your beasts!

The Shepherd

Ba-a!

The Judge [to the Draper]

You show well what you are, sir, by's death!

The Draper

Oh, my lord, upon my soul, I wish . . .

Patelin [to the bystanders]

Could he stop?

The Draper [turning upon Patelin]

And my business is with y o u! You cheated

me and carried off my cloth by stealth and with
your smooth talk . . .

Patelin [*to the Judge*]

I cross my heart! Why, do you hear him, sir?

The Draper [*to Patelin*]

God help me, you're the most arrant trickster . . . [*To the Judge.*] Your Worship, whatever they may say . . .

The Judge

You are a pair of idiots, both of you! It's
naught but wrangling. [*He rises.*] Yah! It is
about time to be leaving. [*To the Shepherd.*] Get
thee gone, my friend, and never return, whatever
bailiff serves a warrant on thee. The court acquits
thee. Dost thou comprehend?

Patelin [*to the Shepherd*]

Say 'I thank you, sir.'

The Shepherd

Ba-a!

The Judge [*to the Shepherd*]

I mean it. Never mind! Begone! [*Half to
himself.*] It is just as well.

[85]

The Draper

Is it fair that he should go away like this?

The Judge [with a snort of disgust]

Huh! I have business elsewhere. [*Both to Patelin and to the Draper.*] You are by all odds too fond of jibes. You shall keep me no longer: I am going. [*To Patelin.*] Will you come and sup with me, Master Pierre?

Patelin [puts his hand over his mouth and winces, as if his teeth were still aching]

I cannot.

[*Exit. Judge, followed by the throng of archers, bailiffs, loiterers, etc.*]

SCENE XIX

(*Still in the market-place*)

THE DRAPER, PATELIN, THE SHEPHERD

The Draper [to Patelin]

A downright robber! that's what you are! Say! Am I going to be paid?

Patelin

For what? Is your mind wandering? Why, who do you think I am? By my heel! I was wondering who you took me for.

The Draper

Pah!

Patelin

My dear sir, wait a bit. I 'll tell you right now who you think you take me for. Maybe it 's for Brainless? [*With one hand Patelin removes his hat; with the other he points to his bald spot.*] Look! [*Deprecatingly.*] Nay, nay! He is n't bald, as I am, on top of his pate.

The Draper

You mean to take me for a blockhead, eh? 'T is you, as sure as I 'm alive, — you yourself. Your voice proves it, and I know it 's so.

Patelin

What! Me myself? Nay; truly it is n't. Try another guess. Might n't it be Jean de Noyon? He 's shaped like me.

The Draper

Ugh! He has no such boozy, sodden face.

[87]

Didn't I leave you sick in bed a short while
since?

Patelin

Ho! There you have it! Sick? And with what
malady? Own up to being a jackanapes, — as
clearly enough you are!

The Draper

It's you; by Saint Peter's bones! You! and
nobody else! I know it for a fact.

Patelin

Now, don't you believe anything of the sort!
For it's not me, at all. I never took an ell, nor
even half an ell, from you. It's likely I would
do such a thing!

The Draper [*looking blank*]

Hm! I'm going to have a look at your house,
to see whether you are there. There's no use in
our worrying our heads about it any longer here,
if I find you there.

Patelin

By'r Lady! Now you have it! That is the
way to find out.

[*Exit Draper.*]

[88]

SCENE XX
(Near the front of the market-place)

Patelin, The Shepherd

Patelin

Say, Lambkin !

The Shepherd

Ba-a !

Patelin [beckoning]

Come hither. Come. Was thy business well done? [*The Shepherd does not move; Patelin starts to approach him*]

The Shepherd [edging off]

Ba-a!

Patelin [stops, apprehensive lest Lambkin may take to flight]

The plaintiff's gone, now. Cease thy *ba-a:* it's no longer needed. [*Winsomely.*] Did n't I trounce him? Did n't I counsel thee just right?

The Shepherd

Ba-a-a !

[89]

Patelin [drawing a step or two closer]

Come, come! Nobody will overhear you. Speak right out. You need n't fear.

The Shepherd [looking for an outlet]

Ba-a!

Patelin [firmly]

It is time for me to be going. Pay me!

The Shepherd [just audibly]

Ba-a!

Patelin [patting the Shepherd, and in a beguiling tone]

To say truth, you did your part prettily, and your behaviour was first rate. What left him in the lurch was the way you kept from laughing.

The Shepherd [bleating a little louder]

Ba-a-a!

Patelin

Why *ba-a?* It 's not needed any longer. [*Holds out his hand.*] Come! Pay me well and nicely.

The Shepherd

Ba-a!

Patelin

Why *ba-a?* Talk sensibly, and pay me; then I will go my way.

[90]

Le Bergier
Bee
Pathelin
Dien ca Bien
ta Besongne est esse Bien faicte
Le Bergier
Bee

Patelin tries to collect his fee

The Shepherd [still louder]

Ba-a-a!

Patelin

Let me tell you something. Can you guess what I am going to say? Please pay me without further railing. I 've had enough of your *ba-a*. [*Holding out his hand.*] Pay me, quick!

The Shepherd [backs off, with a prolonged bleat]

Ba-a-a-a!

Patelin [reproachfully]

Is this mockery? Is this the most you intend to do? [*Growing fiercely eager.*] Upon my oath, you shall pay me, unless you can fly! [*Cornering the Shepherd.*] Do you understand? Here! My fee!

The Shepherd

Ba-a!

Patelin

This is a jest! [*With a shade of pathos*] What! Is this all I am to get?

The Shepherd

Ba-a!

Patelin [half in jest, but persuasively]

You are riming; but this is prose. Hm! Is

[92]

there any green in my eye? Are you aware whom you are trying to take in? Babble to me no longer with your *ba-a!* and pay me my fee.

> *The Shepherd* [*growing restless*]
Ba-a-a!

> *Patelin* [*keeping him cornered*]
Is that the only cash I am to get? With whom do you fancy you are playing? [*Regretfully.*] And I was to take such pride in you! Now let me be proud of you.

> *The Shepherd*
Ba-a!

> *Patelin*
Are you feeding me on goose? [*Fiercely.*] By Gog's arms! Have I lived to see myself jeered at by an oaf, a sheep in clothing, a filthy churl!

> *The Shepherd*
Ba-a!

> *Patelin* [*in gentle reproach*]
Is this the only word I am to hear? If you are merely fooling, say so, and spare me further argument. [*A slight pause.*] Come to my house for supper, Lambkin.

[93]

The Shepherd [*glances at Patelin cunningly ; then
 gives a loud bleat*]

Ba-a-a!

Patelin [*half to himself*]

By Saint John, you are right! The goslings
take the geese to pasture. [*To himself.*] I thought
myself the master of all deceivers, here and elsewhere ; of the old stagers, too, and of such as pay
their debts on Doomsday ; but a mere shepherd
leaves me behind! [*To the Shepherd, who is trying
to make good his escape.*] By Saint James! if I
could find a bailiff, I'd have you nabbed!

The Shepherd [*dodging about, while Patelin endeavours to head him off*]

Ba-a! Ba-a-a!

Patelin [*trying to get hold of the Shepherd*]

Hm! *Ba-a!* Hang me if I don't go after a
good bailiff! Bad luck to him if he does n't put
you into gaol!

The Shepherd [*fleeing*]

If he finds me, I'll forgive him!

EXPLICIT

[94]

NOTES ON THE TEXT

NOTES ON THE TEXT

I

Page 4. 'The Conjuring-book.' Guillemette means *le grimaire*, a derivative of *grammatica* (= 'Latin grammar'). For several centuries the superstitious regarded *le grimaire* (English 'gramary') as a work having some occult connexion with the Devil. See, for instance, the *fabliau* of *Martin Hapart*, vol. ii, p. 176, in the *Recueil général et complet des fabliaux*. In the *fabliau* of *Le roi d'Angleterre et le jongleur d'Ely, ib.,* p. 242, *grymoire* seems to mean 'rigmarole.' In Rabelais (iv, 45) we read: 'Autour de luy estoient trois prebstres bien ras et tonsurés, lisans le *grimoyre* et conjurans les diables.' To give in modern speech the exact connotation of *le grimaire* is quite impossible.

II

Page 4. 'Charlemaine in Spain.' The first verses of the *Song of Roland* state that Charles the Great spent full seven years in Spain.

III

Page 5. 'Slyboots.' Le Roy reads *chaudes testes;* Levet changes *chaudes* to *saiges.* Levet's alteration seems to indicate that *chaudes testes* was no longer clear in 1489, or thereabouts, and had, therefore, to be replaced by a more familiar expression. In my opinion, *chaudes testes* was slang, and meant something not very different from the translation that I have offered. At all

events, to think of this wily barrister as ' hot-headed ' would
be to endow him with a characteristic scarcely in keeping with
his personality as it is portrayed in the remainder of the piece.
A dare-devil he is, but self-controlled. It was trickery, not anger
or violence, that caused Maître Pierre to spend a Saturday in the
pillory.

IV

Page 5. ' Silks and satins,' — a rough equivalent of *camelos*
. . *et* . . *camocas*. Camlet, or chamlet, — to give the English
forms of *camelot* and *chamelot*, — seems to have been a thick,
wavy material, originally composed of camel's hair or goat's hair,
but later, apparently, of silk and wool. ' Of fees and robes
hadde he many oon,' says Chaucer of his Sergeant of the Law,
and Rabelais scoffingly mentions ' l'avocat, seigneur de Came-
lotière,' uncle of ' le medecin d'eau douce, feu Amer ' (Prol.
Book v). *Camoca* was probably a silken stuff, also sumptuous.

Patelin's envious thrust at the gorgeously robed lawyers strikes
home; for they, as well as the half-starved throng of pettifoggers
to which Patelin belongs, were bent upon filling their wallets by
hook or by crook. Commines (vi, 5) was indignant at their
corrupt practices ; generations later they aroused the scorn of
Montaigne and excited the sarcasm of Molière.

V

Page 6. ' [*Counting on his fingers*] ' — the only stage-direction to be found in any known fifteenth-century text of *Patelin*.

VI

Page 8. ' Undergarment.' The original seems to contain a
complicated pun on *blanchet*, which may be taken as the dimin-
utive of *blanc* (English 'blank '), a small coin; or may mean
' blanket' for a bed, or a ' petticoat ' ; or even be the antonym
of *brunet*, the masculine of *brunette*. The actor who performed

the part of Patelin was no doubt made up to look pale (*fade*) and boozy (*potatif*), as we shall see further on (pp. 48 and 87). If Patelin is both pale and boozy, he is *blanchet*. This farce contains several puns of varying merit; but the reader will pardon the translator both for his inability to do them justice, and for passing them henceforth in silence.

VII

Page 17. 'God's-pennies.' The system of giving a tradesman earnest-money still survives; but nowadays we call it a 'deposit,' rather than 'God's-penny,' as it was commonly called by our medieval ancestors.

In the Middle Ages it seems to have been customary to give the God's-penny to the purveyor, or to his agent (see Du Cange), as a token of religious obligation to pay the whole debt within a certain period, — not on Doomsday, in the manner of Master Patelin. Often, if not always, the *denier à Dieu* (*denarius Dei*) was dropped into a box somewhere near the church, or either in or near the market-place. There it remained till removed by a servant of the Church. My stage-direction follows closely the tradition of the Comédie Française, and is probably not a contradiction of history.

VIII

Page 18. 'Saturday.' Market-day regularly fell on Saturday. See Note xiv.

IX

Page 18. 'Saint Maudeleyne's day.' Magdalen College at Oxford, despite its spelling, preserves the Middle English pronunciation. I have chosen the popular form because of its euphonious nature and its more popular, less sacred air. Saint Maudeleyne's day is the 22 July.

X

Page 21. 'That goose.' Patelin says, in the original, 'Et si mengeres de mon oye,' — a grimly humorous phrase ; for, in the first place, Master Pierre has no goose, and, furthermore, *manger de l'oye*, or *de l'oue*, was a proverbial expression, meaning approximately ' to get something not bargained for,' or, as we say, ' to go on a fool's errand,' or on ' a wild-goose chase.' Imagine the pleasure with which an early audience would have listened to this bit of dramatic irony.

XI

Page 24. 'That trickster,' etc. These few words damn the Draper. He makes himself fair game, and his subsequent misfortunes are justified from an artistic point of view, however little they are justified by morality.

XII

Page 27. ' Guillaume.' In the fifteenth century ' Guillaume ' meant not only ' William,' but also ' dunce ' or ' gull.' It would be easy to cite many similar applications of English baptismal names. Jack-pudding, Jackanapes, Tomfool, Willy, Neddy, Johnny (a town fop who haunts green-rooms, or any effeminate man-about-town), Miss Nancy, and Ralph Spooner will do for examples. ' Chaque nation,' says Montaigne (1, 46), ' a quelques noms qui se prennent, je ne sçay comment, en mauvaise part : et à nous Jehan, Guillaume, Benoit.' Montaigne goes on to say that at a banquet given by Henry Duke of Normandy the guests were grouped at table according to their names. At the first table sat one hundred and ten knights named Guillaume.

XIII

Page 27. ' Let's bind the bargain with a drink.' The im-

[100]

plication is obvious; but could Patelin have got any publican to trust him? See page 8 of the text.

XIV

Page 30. 'That Saturday they put you in the stocks.' Saturday was chosen because it was market-day (see Note VIII). The prisoner's ignominy would thus be known, not only to his fellow townsmen, but also to the crowds who flocked in from the neighbouring country. Here we encounter, therefore, one of several flaws or inconsistencies in the plot of *Patelin*. Even so dull a fool as the Draper could hardly be ignorant of Patelin's reputation; indeed he calls him a trickster, as we have seen; nevertheless he trusts Patelin, and actually expects to receive payment and have a bite of Patelin's goose.

XV

Page 31. 'Saint Mat.' Mathurinus was a saint in Gastinois (Gâtinais), a district lying southwest of Paris. Saint Mathelin, to give his popular name, was 'held to be the Physitian, or Patron of mad fooles' (Cotgrave). 'Saint Vitus's dance' is one of the few English phrases left over from a time when various saints supplied names for as many kinds of maladies. The liberty of abbreviating the name has been taken because 'Mathelin' would rime disagreeably (in prose) with 'Patelin,' and because 'Mathelin' is in any case a name without meaning, so far as most persons are concerned.

XVI

Page 38. 'This must have happened since sunrise, then,' etc. On page 68 we learn that the trial takes place about six o'clock. In the fifteenth century the hours had come to be reckoned as they are now. Therefore the whole action of *Patelin* consumes some ten or twelve hours of daylight, and the first great comedy

[101]

composed in a modern tongue observes the Unity of Time, if we understand that term according to traditional canons. In reality the imagination needs only about an hour and a quarter to learn a series of events which occupy, with intervals not altogether easy to determine, a period lasting approximately from rather early in the morning till dusk.

Now, as to the Unity of Place. On the medieval stage the various scenes of a story were visualised, not by the shifting of scenery, but by the juxtaposition of all the structures necessary to the performance of a given piece. From the beginning of a play to its close the stage-setting remained unchanged. Such, at any rate, was the character of the 'serious drama,' and there is no good reason for supposing that a wholly different arrangement obtained in the performing of farces (see Preface, pages xiii and xiv). We may assume that on one side of a broad stage stood the Draper's shop, or some structure intended to represent it. On the other side stood Patelin's abode, designated, perhaps, by hardly more than a wall with a door in it (see the woodcut, page 33), and that this door opened upon an area representing a market-place, or, at all events, a space wide enough to lend some plausibility to the events set forth in *Patelin*. If we grant this to be true, the Unity of Place, also, is observed in *Patelin*. The setting adopted by the Comédie Française is unquestionably very different from that of the Middle Ages, and does not observe the Unity of Place, if by that term we mean one and the same locality completely visible at a given moment.

In *Patelin* the Unity of Action is not marred by any irrelevant digression, though certain entrances are too timely. But this same flaw is common in Molière, whose characters often appear on the scene with no better warrant than a ' Mais le voilà qui vient,' or some other similar phrase. As late as Labiche unjustified entrances are still common; but the most modern playwrights, when they are genuine artists, avoid this defect in dramatic construction.

XVII

Page 39. ' Rosewater,' etc. In the Middle Ages rosewater was supposed to be efficacious in restoring persons who felt faint, or who had fallen into a swoon. Recipes for distilling this remedy have been preserved by numerous works on medicine.

In his essay ' On Three Good Women ' (II, 35), Montaigne speaks of rubbing the feet as if that had been a common way of restoring life or vitality.

XVIII

Page 40. ' Marmara, carimari, carimara.' This gibberish seems to parody some weird formula once used by priests in performing exorcisms upon persons supposedly possessed. We have much the same sort of thing in the mild incantation ' Ena, mena, mina, mo ! Catch a nigger by the toe,' etc., or in ' Fe, fi, fo, fum ! I smell the blood of an Englishmun !' As Patelin is being plagued by ' black men,' the conjecture that ' marmara, carimari, carimara ' is a burlesque of some formula of exorcism, seems highly plausible, though these particular syllables may imitate some rigmarole in the patter of fifteenth-century trick-performing mounte-banks.

XIX

Page 40. ' Away with them! away!' The text reads, ' Amenes les moy, amenes!' In the so-called *Chronique scan-daleuse* (A. D. 1460–1483), and in various other medieval texts, *amener* is more than once used for *emmener*. My translation is warranted, therefore, by pure philology as well as by common sense.

XX

Page 40. ' A stole.' When a priest had occasion to drive away the devil, it was desirable, if not indispensable, that he should use a stole, the symbol of obedience. For a detailed description of this custom, which is still common in the Roman Catholic Church, see my 'Exorcism with a Stole,' in *Modern Language Notes* for December, 1904.

XXI

Page 42. 'My water.' Medieval physicians set great store by the examination of urinal symptoms. A large number of manuscripts treating of this subject have come down, and literary allusions are common as late as the eighteenth century.

XXII

Page 44. 'No goose.' At this period geese were a luxury not often relished by persons like our Draper, and one may imagine how he had set his heart on eating this delicacy at Patelin's table. See Note x.

XXIII

Page 48. 'Three lessons and three psalms.' Between the eleventh and fourteenth centuries the Franciscans began to feel that the Breviary required them to recite too many lessons and too many psalms. So they reduced the number from nine to three, — at least, on certain occasions only three lessons and three psalms were required. In the thirteenth century it became customary in France to recite only three psalms at matins throughout Easter, nor was this easy-going way characteristic merely of the Abbey of Fécamp, as a famous passage in Rabelais might lead us to suppose. ' "According to what usage," said Gargantua [to the monk], "do you say these beautiful hours?" — "According to the usage of Fécamp," said the monk, "with three lessons and three psalms, or, for those who are unwilling, nothing at all." ' (*Gargantua*, I, 41.)

Before the days of printing, breviaries were so costly that they were often chained to a bench in the choir, and each monk or priest had to learn the minimum by heart. That those who knew only the minimum should have excited the pity or scorn of their more diligent brethren, and that their feelings should have been expressed in such a manner as to give rise to this proverbial taunt, is not contrary to the tendencies of human nature. The Draper could hardly have hit upon a more ludicrously appropriate phrase to express his contemptuous indignation and his self-esteem.

XXIV

Page 50. 'The Abbot of Ivernaux.' The Abbey of Ivernaux, or Hivernaux, was situate near the hamlet called Brie-Comte-Robert, which lies some twenty miles southeast of Paris, in whose archbishopric was the Church of Ivernaux. The Abbey of Ivernaux was sadly weakened by the wars of the fourteenth and fifteenth centuries.

But to what Abbot of Ivernaux is Patelin alluding ?

In a lease dated 1441, and in another dated 1451, one Nicolas Bottelin is spoken of as 'abbot.' Another lease, dated 1461, applies the title to a Jean d'Arquevilliers. Philippe seems to have been the name of an Abbot of Ivernaux who signed a lease on 31 March, 1468.

Whatever may be the advantage of knowing these names, — very barren things at best, — it is worth our while to learn that in 1468, the year before *Patelin* first entered an extant record, the Abbot of Ivernaux was no longer a power, for his abbacy had sunk into poverty ; yet even a certain wealth and influence would hardly have saved the Abbot of Ivernaux from being the butt of Patelin's somewhat lewd jocularity, and we may be sure that our lawyer in his sham delirium was not shooting an arrow at the moon. The abbot was doubtless a gay fellow, and a worthy contemporary of Huguette du Hamel, who, notwithstanding her intimacy with François Villon and other reprobates, and although she had been guilty of inciting a hireling to murder, could still hold her position as Abbess of Port-Royal. Yet the real importance of this allusion to the Abbot of Ivernaux is that it seems to show that our farce was composed to be performed in the region round about Brie-Comte-Robert ; for it is unlikely that this particular abbot's fame had spread very far beyond the bounds of his abbacy.

XXV

Page 51. ' Mere de diou,' etc. In this and the following passages of dialect or jargon the translator was confronted by a problem of serious difficulty. Three courses seemed possible : (*a*) to transform *Patelin* into an out-and-out English farce, changing the names of the characters, and transplanting the scene to medieval England ; (*b*) to preserve the point of Guillemette's explanations by leaving Patelin's *reveries* untranslated ; (*c*) to adopt the plan chosen by Albrecht Count Wickenburg, who, in his excellent verse-translation into German (Vienna, 1883), leaves no foreign words save the Latin, substituting for the other dialects and jargons certain passages of his own invention, in which Patelin is made to rave, now like a delirious alchemist who talks incoherently of quicksilver, sulphur, etc., or like a dying man who pretends to see the flames of hell, as well as other phenomena unnecessary to mention.

Similar approximations will be found in Fournier's version (1871) and in a later (undated) version by Eudoxie Dupuis. The present translation, however, aims at the highest degree of literality consistent with the use of idiomatic, comprehensible English, and aims, furthermore, to be loyal to what is not merely a farce, but also a document of historical importance. I doubt that the retention of these passages will destroy the reader's illusion : he will probably understand the obscurest of them quite as well as they were understood by *Patelin's* first audience ; the others will simply be somewhat less intelligible than they seemed to Frenchmen in 1469. It may be added that the author of Patelin has made these passages so long as to render them rather boresome *from a modern point of view ;* for, even if one understands them pretty well, they lack a certain charm which brevity imparts. I have not hesitated, therefore, to shorten them slightly ; but a comparison with any fifteenth-century edition will show the reader how the cutting was done. It seemed undesirable to attempt here in the Notes what would be a fragmentary and not very interesting series of translations.

XXVI

Page 54. ' But how does he come to speak Norman.' Not in the original; added for clearness.

XXVII

Page 57. ' Quid.' *Qui* in the original. A mistake due, perhaps, to the fact that *d* final in French is generally silent.

XXVIII

Page 57. The original text of Guillemette's speech is corrupt. My translation is based on a temporary attempt at restoration.

XXIX

Page 58. ' How do you like me for a teacher ? ' — in the original, *Avant vous ay je bien aprins.* Fifteenth-century syntax allows a so-called masculine past participle to go with a feminine antecedent. *Vous* means not the Draper, but Guillemette.

XXX

Page 59. The long stage-direction describes how this episode of *Patelin* is wound up at the Comédie Française. The medieval stage had no curtain, and we have no means of knowing how Patelin and Guillemette made themselves inconspicuous at the close of this scene.

XXXI

Page 60. ' *The Shepherd.*' The Shepherd's entrance is too timely. Nothing in the plot warrants his appearance at precisely this instant. Similar unjustified entrances are common in Molière, who, as has been said (Note XVI), often uses some stock formula to keep a character from seeming to blunder in.

XXXII

Page 60. 'Some one or other in striped hosen.' This was a *Sergent à verge*, an officer empowered to make arrests, effect seizures, etc.

XXXIII

Page 62. 'By Saint Lupus.' The Shepherd's oath is well chosen ; for wolves were still a pest at this period. Saint Lupus (Saint Wolf, to translate his name) was called Saint Leu in Old French. As late as 1633 there was standing near that Noyon which is mentioned on page 87 a monastery dedicated to Saint Leu, who was honoured, also, at Troyes in Champagne.

XXXIV

Page 64. 'A dealer.' The Shepherd does not name the ' dealer ' ; Patelin, on his side, neglects, or the dramatist, for his own convenience or through carelessness, neglects to have Patelin inquire as to the dealer's identity. So Patelin, on arriving at the trial, is astonished to confront the very individual whom he has himself cheated. The Draper, as we have seen, had lied to Patelin by telling him that his whole flock had perished in the great frost (page 18). That our crafty lawyer should fail to make the Shepherd divulge his master's name seems incredible ; it is to this flaw in characterisation that we owe one of the most comic features of the trial scene, namely the unexpected meeting of the Lawyer and his dupe.

XXXV

Page 67. 'Answer nothing but *ba-a*,' etc. In the second
part of his edition of *A C. Mery Tales and Quicke Answers*
(*Shakespere Jest Books*, page 60), Mr. W. Carew Hazlitt has
reprinted the anecdote 'Of hym that payde his dette with crienge
bea.' In this version the Shepherd is replaced by a spendthrift;
otherwise the anecdote is nothing more nor less than a kind of
disguised summary of the plot of *Patelin* from verse 1067 (in
this translation, from Scene XVII) to the end. Whether this particular anecdote figured in the edition of the *C. Mery Tales*
printed by John Rastell about 1525, Mr. Hazlitt does not say.
It entered, at all events, into the collection printed by Thomas
Berthelet about 1535. Assuming this date to be nearly correct,
we may assert that our French farce must have been known in
England a century before Rabelais. It was, therefore, not through
Rabelais that *Patelin* began to influence English literature.

The legal episodes of *Patelin*, as they appear in the *C. Mery
Tales*, might be conceived to occur at almost any time and in
almost any country; for no names are given. In *Pasquil's Jests*
(see Hazlitt, *op. cit.*, vol. III, pp. 45, 46), of which several
editions were printed in the first half of the seventeenth century,
we find almost exactly the same story, slightly shortened and
with the scene laid in London. The version in *Pasquil's Jests*
is derived, without doubt, from the earlier English version, and
not from the French text. There can be no question of folklore
in this matter: what we have is a loan, made through a literary
channel.

To sum up: The last third of *Patelin* was epitomised for English readers in the first third of the sixteenth century. But, to go
further, I will venture the opinion that *Patelin*, in one or more
of the many editions printed in France and in the fifteenth century, had crossed the Channel before 1500, and it was no doubt

from one of these original texts that some more or less literary person derived his summary. Yet it was probably through Rabelais that the wily Patelin became known for the first time to a considerable number of people in England. See Introduction, page xxxvi ff.

XXXVI

Page 69. 'Welcome, sir!' The Judge has no reason to suppose that Patelin has a client, but he knows that lawyer. See the beginning of the piece and notice that the Judge invites Patelin to supper (page 86).

XXXVII

Page 75. 'Come! Let's stick to those sheep!' 'Sus! Revenons à ces moutons!' cries the Judge, and he coins one of those neat and useful phrases which soon make their way from country to country, entering the every-day speech of persons quite unaware to whom or what they are indebted. In his essay on Marlowe (*Old English Dramatists*) James Russell Lowell says, ' But it is high time that I should remember Maître Guillaume of *Patelin*, and return to my sheep.' The mention of ' Guillaume ' indicates that Lowell had read *Patelin*, and that he was not merely borrowing the words ' to return to our sheep ' from Rabelais. In the first chapter of *Gargantua*, Rabelais says, ' Retournant à nos moutons, je vous dis . . .'; but it is likely that the *nos* had been substituted for the less convenient *ces* (a homonym of *ses*) a good while before Rabelais read *Patelin*. Owing to facetiousness rather than to ignorance, *moutons* is usually rendered not by ' sheep,' but by ' muttons,' — a mistranslation which neatly indicates the proverb's Gallic origin.

XXXVIII

Page 87. 'Brainless' (Esservelé) figured, no doubt, in some farce or morality no longer extant. In ' Mr. Golightly,' ' Dobbin,' etc., not to mention many allegorical names in the older comedy, English furnishes parallels.

XXXIX

Page 87. Of Jean de Noyon nothing is known save what we may infer from the text of *Patelin*. Assuredly he was a real character, contemporary with the audience for which *Patelin* was first performed, and one may surmise that he was more or less notorious, and that he bore a strong, perhaps a comic, likeness to the actor who first played the part of Patelin. But this is guess-work. Whatever the truth may be, it is highly improbable that this Jean belonged to the noble family having its seat at Noyon ; for this family seems to have died out before the fifteenth century ; nor do I find a Jean de Noyon among the few Fools whose names have been handed down.

XL

Page 89. Why has the Shepherd remained ? Simply to fur-nish another scene, one of the best scenes of all ; but obviously Lambkin had a good chance to escape when the Judge dismissed him. In real life so canny a rogue would not fail to make him-self scarce as soon as possible.

XLI

Page 94. Here occurs the first bit of moralising in *Patelin ;* but the Lawyer is not repentant ; he is crestfallen at being outwitted by a shepherd : that is all. His chagrin is followed by a touch of anger, yet it is only a touch, and we may fancy a sardonic grin passing over his lean countenance as he looks again at the 'sheep in clothing' who has so admirably carried out his own instructions.

Genuine moralisations, such as one finds in the younger Du-mas and in certain plays by Mr. Bernard Shaw, are exceedingly rare in the old French farces.

XLII

Page 94. ' If he finds me, I 'll forgive him ! ' These are the
last words in all the old editions. They break the Shepherd's
promise (page 67), but our dramatist, knowing human nature
and drawing it with a sure hand, leaves his work with no weak
or awkward ending. It is a skilful stroke to have the Shepherd
behave like a man, after he has so ably behaved like a sheep.
What becomes of him ? We imagine that he continues his mis-
deeds till, after a while, he is nabbed, brought to book, and, having no Patelin to defend him, is properly hanged.

NOTES ON THE CUTS

NOTES ON THE CUTS

THE edition of *Patelin* published by Génin in 1854 contains inaccurate reproductions of five of Levet's illustrative woodcuts: to wit, the first, second, third, fourth, and sixth. But with characteristic whimsicality — or carelessness — Génin borrowed the first and fourth from an inferior edition of *Patelin* by Jehan Treperel.* The trial scene Génin got from Beneaut's *Patelin* (A. D. 1490), though he could have copied the original cut in Levet's edition. Beneaut's two almost identical cuts of the trial scene were not made from the block used by Levet, as some writers have stated ; for Levet's cut has not the same dimensions as the two in Beneaut's edition.

In 1870 Baillieu, 'marchant libraire sur le quay des grâds augustins a Paris,' to quote his pseudo-archaic colophon, published in the so-called 'Bibliothèque gothique' what he apparently intended to pass off as a facsimile, or, at any rate, as a reprint of Levet's *Patelin*. Not only does Baillieu's edition contain many gross textual blunders, but it so distorts Levet's cuts as to give

---

* The Treperel *Patelin*, from which Génin seems to have borrowed his cuts, must have appeared after 13 October, 1499 ; for its colophon reads thus : *Imprime a Paris par Jehan treperel demourant a la rue sainct iacques pres sainct yues a lymaige saint laurens.* Treperel had been obliged to remove to the above address after the fall of the Pont Nostre Dame on the 13 October, 1499.

[115]

a wholly false impression. In a word, Baillieu's *Patelin* is an out-and-out imposture and even worse than worthless.

Inasmuch as no one else has attempted in modern times, in so far as I am aware, to reproduce Levet's woodcuts, the facsimiles in this volume can rightly be called the first that have ever been made. They differ from the originals in the respect that no attempt has been made to imitate Levet's paper, or to reproduce the marks of age. Certain imperfections in Levet's cuts indicate, apparently, either that the only known exemplar of his edition was one of the last to be printed, or that the paper was not properly wetted. I may add that Levet's sixth illustration, to judge by the Shepherd's beard and other inconsistencies of drawing, can hardly have been made by the engraver who executed the other illustrations. See the Preface, page xiii.

The printer's mark of Pierre Levet appears on the first page of his *Patelin*, and serves as a frontispiece to the present volume. Levet did not use the same block when he put this mark in his edition of Villon in 1489.

As to the value of Levet's illustrations of *Patelin*, see the Preface, pages ix and xiii.

Levet's seven woodcuts are here reproduced by permission of M. Léopold Delisle, former Head Librarian of the Bibliothèque Nationale.

The Riverside Press

Electrotyped and printed by H. O. Houghton & Co.
Cambridge, Mass., U. S. A.

Printed in the United States
123905LV00004B/164/A